# MASTERING COMMUNICATION IN THE WORKPLACE

Transform Your Career with
Powerful Communication Skills
Your Boss Never Tought You

Ashlie Ryan

**Girl on Fire Publishing**

Copyright © 2024 Girl on Fire Publishing

This work was created with the assistance of artificial intelligence.

All rights reserved. No part of this book may be reproduced or used in any manner without written permission of the copyright owner except for the use of quotations in a book review.

First Edition, 2024

# CONTENTS

Title Page
Copyright
Chapter 1   1
Chapter 2   7
Chapter 3   13
Chapter 4   21
Chapter 5   29
Chapter 6   39
Chapter 7   48
Chapter 8   56
Chapter 9   67
Chapter 10   77
Chapter 11   88
Reference   99

# CHAPTER 1

# Understanding Emotional Intelligence: The Foundation of Effective Communication

In today's fast-paced and interconnected workplace, technical skills and intelligence quotient (IQ) are no longer sufficient to guarantee success. As organizations become more team-oriented and globalized, a new type of intelligence has emerged as a critical factor in professional achievement: Emotional Intelligence (EI).

## What Is Emotional Intelligence?

Emotional Intelligence, often abbreviated as EI or EQ (Emotional Quotient), refers to the ability to recognize, understand, and manage our own emotions, as well as to recognize, understand, and influence the emotions of others. In essence, it's about how we navigate the complex world of feelings - both our own and those of the people around us.

The concept of EI was popularized in the mid-1990s by psychologist Daniel Goleman, although its roots can be traced back to earlier work by researchers Peter Salovey and John Mayer. Goleman's 1995 book, "Emotional Intelligence: Why It Can Matter More Than IQ," brought the idea into the mainstream, arguing that EI plays a crucial role in personal and professional success.

## The Four Core Components Of Emotional Intelligence

Emotional Intelligence comprises four fundamental components:

1. **Self-awareness**: The ability to recognize and understand your own emotions, strengths, weaknesses, values, and motivations, and how they affect your thoughts and behavior.
2. **Self-management**: The capacity to control or redirect disruptive emotions and impulses, adapt to changing circumstances, and maintain a positive outlook.
3. **Social awareness**: The skill of perceiving and understanding the emotions of others, organizational dynamics, and the ability to empathize with people from diverse backgrounds.
4. **Relationship management**: The proficiency in inspiring, influencing, and developing others, managing conflict, and fostering teamwork.

These components are interconnected and build upon each other. For instance, strong self-awareness forms the foundation for effective self-management and social awareness, which in turn enable skillful relationship management.

## The Importance Of Emotional Intelligence In The Workplace

In professional settings, Emotional Intelligence plays a pivotal role in various aspects:

1. **Leadership**: Leaders with high EI can inspire and motivate their teams more effectively, create a positive work environment, and navigate complex interpersonal dynamics.
2. **Teamwork**: EI facilitates better collaboration, as team members with high EI can communicate more effectively, resolve conflicts constructively, and create a supportive atmosphere.
3. **Customer Relations**: In client-facing roles, EI helps in understanding and meeting customer needs, handling complaints gracefully, and building long-term relationships.
4. **Adaptability**: In times of change or crisis, individuals with high EI are better equipped to manage stress, remain flexible, and guide others through uncertainty.
5. **Decision Making**: EI contributes to more balanced decision-making by helping individuals consider both logical and emotional factors.

## Emotional Intelligence Versus Intelligence Quotient And Technical Skills

While IQ and technical expertise are undoubtedly important, research suggests that EI is often a stronger predictor of success, especially in leadership roles. A high IQ can help you get hired, but it's EI that helps you advance in your career.

Consider this: Technical skills are threshold capabilities - they're the basic requirements for entry into a field. But once you're in, what distinguishes star performers from average ones is often their level of Emotional Intelligence.

This doesn't mean that IQ and technical skills are unimportant. Rather, they work in tandem with EI. The most effective professionals possess a mix of cognitive intelligence, technical expertise, and Emotional Intelligence.

## The Neuroscience Of Emotions And Decision-Making

Recent advances in neuroscience have provided fascinating insights into the role of emotions in decision-making. Contrary to the old belief that emotions interfere with rational thinking, we now know that emotions are integral to sound judgment.

The amygdala, a part of the brain's limbic system, plays a crucial role in processing emotions. It's connected to the prefrontal cortex, which is responsible for executive functions like planning and decision-making. This connection allows emotional input to influence our choices and behavior.

In fact, studies of patients with damage to their emotional processing areas show that they struggle to make even simple decisions. This suggests that emotions provide vital information that guides our reasoning process.

Understanding this interplay between emotions and cognition is crucial for developing Emotional Intelligence. It helps us appreciate why managing our emotions - and understanding those of others - is so important in workplace interactions and decision-making processes.

## Measuring Emotional Intelligence

Unlike IQ, which has standardized tests, measuring EI can be more complex. However, several assessment tools have been developed:

1. **Self-report tests**: These ask individuals to rate their own EI-related abilities.
2. **360-degree assessments**: These gather feedback from colleagues, supervisors, and subordinates to provide a

comprehensive view of an individual's EI.
3. **Ability-based tests**: These present scenarios and ask individuals to solve emotional problems, similar to traditional intelligence tests.

It's important to note that no single test can perfectly capture all aspects of Emotional Intelligence. Often, a combination of methods provides the most accurate picture.

## Challenges In Developing Emotional Intelligence

While EI can be improved over time, it's not without its challenges:

1. **Self-perception**: It can be difficult to accurately assess our own emotional states and behaviors.
2. **Ingrained habits**: Changing emotional responses that have been reinforced over years can be challenging.
3. **Cultural factors**: Different cultures may value and express emotions differently, which can complicate EI development in diverse workplaces.
4. **Time and effort**: Like any skill, developing EI requires consistent practice and patience.

## Conclusion: The Path Forward

As we've seen, Emotional Intelligence is a crucial factor in workplace success. It underpins effective communication, strong leadership, and harmonious team dynamics. Throughout this book, we'll explore each component of EI in depth, providing practical strategies to enhance your emotional intelligence and apply it in various workplace scenarios.

Remember, developing EI is a journey, not a destination. It requires self-reflection, practice, and a willingness to learn from both successes and setbacks. But the rewards - in terms of personal growth, professional achievement, and more fulfilling relationships - are well worth the effort.

In the next chapter, we'll dive deeper into the first component of EI: self-awareness. We'll explore techniques for recognizing and understanding your own emotions, and how this awareness can transform your workplace interactions and performance.

# CHAPTER 2

# Self-Awareness: Recognizing Your Own Emotions in the Workplace

In the previous chapter, we explored the foundations of Emotional Intelligence (EI) and its importance in the workplace. Now, we'll delve into the first and perhaps most crucial component of EI: self-awareness. As the cornerstone of emotional intelligence, self-awareness forms the basis for all other EI competencies and plays a pivotal role in effective workplace communication.

## Understanding Self-Awareness

Self-awareness, in the context of emotional intelligence, refers to the ability to recognize and understand your own emotions, thoughts, and values, as well as their impact on your behavior and decisions. It involves a continuous process of introspection and reflection, allowing you to develop a clear and honest view of yourself.

In professional settings, self-awareness enables you to:

- Recognize how your emotions influence your work performance
- Understand your strengths and limitations
- Identify your values and motivations
- Recognize how others perceive you

## The Components Of Emotional Self-Awareness

Emotional self-awareness comprises several key elements:

1. **Recognizing different types of emotions**: This involves identifying and naming the emotions you experience, from basic feelings like happiness or anger to more complex emotions like frustration or anticipation.
2. **Understanding emotional triggers**: Identifying the events, situations, or interactions that prompt specific emotional responses in you.
3. **Identifying personal patterns of emotional responses**: Recognizing recurring emotional reactions to certain types of situations or people.

## Techniques For Developing Self-Awareness

Enhancing your self-awareness is a continuous process. Here are some effective techniques:

1. **Mindfulness and meditation**: These practices help you become more attuned to your thoughts and feelings in the present moment. Try starting with just 5-10 minutes of mindfulness meditation daily.
2. **Journaling**: Regular reflection through writing can help you track your emotional patterns and responses over time. Consider keeping a daily emotion log.
3. **Seeking feedback**: Actively ask for input from colleagues, supervisors, and mentors about your

behavior and its impact on others. 360-degree feedback processes can be particularly insightful.
4. **Self-assessment tools**: Utilize emotional intelligence assessments or personality inventories to gain structural insights into your emotional tendencies.

## Overcoming Barriers To Self-Awareness In The Workplace

Several factors can hinder the development of self-awareness in professional settings:

1. **Time pressure and stress**: The fast-paced nature of many workplaces can make it challenging to pause and reflect on your emotions.
2. **Ego and defense mechanisms**: Fear of acknowledging weaknesses or mistakes can lead to self-deception.
3. **Organizational culture**: Some workplace environments may discourage emotional expression or introspection.

To overcome these barriers, it's crucial to prioritize self-reflection, create a personal development plan, and seek out environments that value emotional intelligence.

## The Impact Of Self-Awareness On Workplace Performance

Cultivating self-awareness can significantly enhance your professional effectiveness:

1. **Improved decision-making**: Understanding your emotions helps you make more balanced, thoughtful decisions.
2. **Enhanced stress management**: Recognizing stress triggers allows you to develop more effective coping strategies.

3. **Better leadership skills**: Self-aware leaders are often more empathetic, adaptable, and inspiring to their teams.
4. **Increased emotional regulation**: Awareness of your emotional states is the first step in managing them effectively.

## Recognizing And Managing Emotional Hijacks

An emotional hijack occurs when your emotions overwhelm your rational thinking, leading to impulsive reactions. In the workplace, these can be particularly detrimental. Signs of an emotional hijack include:

- Intense physical reactions (rapid heartbeat, flushing)
- Disproportionate emotional responses
- Difficulty concentrating or thinking clearly

To manage emotional hijacks:

1. Learn to recognize the early signs
2. Use techniques like deep breathing or counting to interrupt the emotional surge
3. Remove yourself from the triggering situation if possible
4. Reflect on the incident afterwards to better understand your triggers

## The Role Of Self-Awareness In Managing Workplace Relationships

Self-awareness is fundamental to effective interpersonal relationships at work:

1. **Understanding your communication style**: Recognizing how you tend to express yourself helps you

adapt your communication to different colleagues and situations.
2. **Recognizing your impact on others**: Being aware of how your moods and behaviors affect those around you allows you to create a more positive work environment.
3. **Improving conflict resolution skills**: Understanding your own emotional responses in conflicts helps you approach disagreements more constructively.

## Developing An Accurate Self-Image

A key aspect of self-awareness is cultivating an accurate self-image:

1. **Balancing self-confidence and humility**: Recognize your strengths without overestimating them, and acknowledge areas for improvement without undue self-criticism.
2. **Seeking diverse perspectives**: Gather feedback from a wide range of colleagues to get a comprehensive view of your workplace persona.
3. **Regularly reassessing your self-view**: As you grow and develop, your self-image should evolve too.

## Practical Exercises To Improve Self-Awareness

1. **Daily emotion check-ins**: Take a few moments each day to identify and name your current emotional state.
2. **Emotion-mapping technique**: Create a "map" of your emotional responses to common workplace situations.
3. **Partner exercises**: Work with a trusted colleague to give each other regular, honest feedback on observed behaviors and their impacts.

## Conclusion: Integrating Self-Awareness Into Your

## Professional Life

Developing self-awareness is an ongoing journey that requires commitment and practice. By consistently applying the techniques and exercises outlined in this chapter, you can enhance your emotional self-awareness and, in turn, improve your overall emotional intelligence.

Remember, self-awareness is not just about understanding yourself—it's about leveraging that understanding to become more effective in your professional interactions and decision-making. As you progress in your self-awareness journey, you'll likely find that it not only enhances your workplace performance but also contributes to greater job satisfaction and personal growth.

In the next chapter, we'll explore how to build upon self-awareness to develop effective self-management strategies, allowing you to channel your emotions productively in the workplace.

# CHAPTER 3

# Self-Regulation: Managing Your Emotions for Professional Success

In the previous chapters, we explored the foundations of Emotional Intelligence (EI) and delved into self-awareness. Now, we turn our attention to the critical skill of self-regulation – the ability to manage and control our emotions, particularly in challenging workplace situations.

## Introduction To Self-Regulation

Self-regulation, in the context of emotional intelligence, refers to the capacity to manage our emotions and behaviors in ways that lead to positive outcomes. It's about choosing how we react to our emotions rather than being controlled by them. In the workplace, effective self-regulation can mean the difference between a composed, respected professional and one who is viewed as volatile or unreliable.

The link between self-awareness and self-regulation is crucial. While self-awareness helps us recognize our emotions, self-regulation allows us to manage them effectively. Think of self-awareness as the diagnosis and self-regulation as the treatment.

## Components Of Emotional Self-Regulation

Emotional self-regulation comprises several key components:

1. **Impulse Control**: The ability to resist or delay an impulse, drive, or temptation to act.
2. **Adaptability**: The capacity to adapt to changing situations and overcome obstacles.
3. **Achievement Orientation**: The drive to meet or exceed a standard of excellence.
4. **Positive Outlook**: The ability to maintain hope and resilience, even in the face of setbacks.

## The Neurophysiology Of Emotional Regulation

Understanding the brain science behind emotional regulation can provide valuable insights into why we react the way we do and how we can better manage our responses.

The prefrontal cortex, often called the "executive center" of the brain, plays a crucial role in emotional regulation. It helps us plan, make decisions, and moderate our behavior. The amygdala, on the other hand, is our emotional alarm system, quickly processing and responding to potential threats.

When we experience strong emotions, the amygdala can override the prefrontal cortex, leading to impulsive reactions. Self-regulation techniques often work by strengthening the connection between the prefrontal cortex and the amygdala, allowing our "rational" brain to modulate our emotional responses.

## Common Workplace Triggers And Emotional

## Reactions

Workplace environments are rife with potential emotional triggers. Some common ones include:

- Criticism or negative feedback
- Tight deadlines or high-pressure situations
- Conflicts with colleagues or superiors
- Feelings of being undervalued or overlooked
- Unexpected changes or uncertainties

These triggers can lead to a range of emotional reactions, from anger and frustration to anxiety and disappointment. Recognizing your personal triggers is the first step in developing effective self-regulation strategies.

## Strategies For Improving Emotional Self-Regulation

1. **Cognitive Reframing**: This involves changing how you think about a situation. For example, instead of seeing criticism as a personal attack, view it as an opportunity for growth.
2. **Mindfulness and Meditation**: Regular mindfulness practice can enhance your ability to observe your emotions without immediately reacting to them.
3. **Physical Techniques**:
    - Deep breathing: Simple deep breathing exercises can help calm your nervous system.
    - Progressive muscle relaxation: Systematically tensing and relaxing muscle groups can reduce physical and mental tension.
4. **Time Management and Organization**: Often, stress and negative emotions arise from feeling overwhelmed. Improving your time management skills can reduce these triggers.

5. **Emotional Labeling**: Putting a name to your emotions can help you gain some distance and control over them.

## The Impact Of Stress On Self-Regulation

Chronic stress can significantly impair our ability to self-regulate. Under stress, our body's fight-or-flight response is activated, making it harder to think clearly and control our reactions.

To manage stress effectively:

- Practice regular stress-reduction techniques (exercise, meditation, hobbies)
- Prioritize sleep and maintain a healthy diet
- Set clear boundaries between work and personal life
- Seek support when needed, whether from colleagues, mentors, or mental health professionals

## Emotional Regulation In Conflict Situations

Conflicts are inevitable in any workplace, and they often test our self-regulation skills to the limit. Here are some strategies for maintaining composure during disagreements:

1. **Pause before responding**: Take a moment to breathe and collect your thoughts.
2. **Use "I" statements**: Express your feelings without blaming others.
3. **Practice active listening**: Truly hearing others can de-escalate tensions.
4. **Seek common ground**: Look for areas of agreement as a starting point.

## The Role Of Self-Regulation In Decision-Making

Emotions play a significant role in decision-making, but

unchecked emotions can lead to poor choices. Self-regulation helps us balance emotion and reason:

1. **Recognize emotional influences**: Be aware of how your current emotional state might be affecting your judgment.
2. **Create distance**: For important decisions, give yourself time to let initial emotional reactions subside.
3. **Consider multiple perspectives**: This can help counteract emotional biases.
4. **Use structured decision-making tools**: Frameworks like pros-and-cons lists can add objectivity to emotionally charged decisions.

## Cultural Aspects Of Emotional Self-Regulation

Cultural norms significantly influence how emotions are expressed and regulated in the workplace. What's considered appropriate emotional expression in one culture might be seen as excessive or insufficient in another.

In diverse workplaces:

- Be aware of cultural differences in emotional expression
- Avoid making assumptions about others' emotional states based on your cultural norms
- Strive for clear, explicit communication about expectations and interpretations

## Self-Regulation And Professional Boundaries

Maintaining appropriate emotional boundaries is crucial for professional relationships:

1. **Empathy with limits**: While it's important to be empathetic, avoid taking on others' emotional burdens.
2. **Confidentiality**: Respect the privacy of emotionally

charged information shared by colleagues.
3. **Personal vs. Professional**: Be mindful of sharing personal emotional issues in professional settings.

## The Connection Between Self-Regulation And Resilience

Self-regulation is a key component of resilience – the ability to bounce back from setbacks. By managing our emotional responses to failures and challenges, we can maintain a sense of perspective and continue moving forward.

To build resilience:

- View setbacks as opportunities for learning and growth
- Maintain a support network of colleagues and mentors
- Regularly acknowledge and celebrate your successes, no matter how small

## Emotional Labor And Its Impact On Self-Regulation

Emotional labor – the process of managing feelings and expressions to fulfill the emotional requirements of a job – can be particularly draining. This is especially true in service-oriented professions.

To manage the toll of emotional labor:

- Schedule regular breaks to recharge
- Develop clear transitions between work and personal time
- Practice self-compassion and acknowledge the challenges of your work

## Technology And Emotional Self-Regulation

Digital communication can both help and hinder emotional self-regulation:

- **Challenges**: The immediacy of digital communication can lead to hasty, emotional responses.
- **Opportunities**: Digital tools can provide a buffer, allowing time for emotional regulation before responding.

Tips for digital emotional regulation:

- Implement a "cooling off" period before sending important emails
- Be mindful of the limitations of text-based communication in conveying emotion
- Use emotion-tracking apps to increase your emotional awareness

## Practical Exercises For Enhancing Self-Regulation Skills

1. **Emotion Logging**: Keep a daily log of emotional triggers and your responses.
2. **Scenario Practice**: Mentally rehearse your response to challenging situations.
3. **Partner Feedback**: Work with a trusted colleague to give each other feedback on emotional regulation.
4. **Mindfulness Minutes**: Practice short mindfulness exercises throughout the workday.

## Measuring Progress In Emotional Self-Regulation

Tracking your progress in self-regulation can provide motivation and insights:

- Use self-assessment tools to periodically evaluate your emotional control

- Keep a journal of how you handle emotionally challenging situations
- Seek feedback from colleagues on noticeable changes in your emotional management

## Conclusion: Integrating Self-Regulation Into Daily Professional Life

Developing strong self-regulation skills is a journey, not a destination. It requires consistent practice and self-reflection. As you continue to enhance your self-regulation abilities, you'll likely find that you're better equipped to handle workplace challenges, make sound decisions, and build strong professional relationships.

Remember, the goal isn't to suppress emotions, but to manage them effectively. Emotions, when properly regulated, can be a source of energy, creativity, and connection in the workplace.

In the next chapter, we'll explore how to build upon self-awareness and self-regulation to develop empathy – the ability to understand and share the feelings of others, which is crucial for effective workplace relationships and leadership.

# CHAPTER 4

# Empathy: The Key to Building Strong Professional Relationships

In our journey through the components of Emotional Intelligence, we've explored self-awareness and self-regulation. Now, we turn our attention outward to a critical skill that bridges the gap between self and others: empathy. In the workplace, empathy is not just a "nice-to-have" trait; it's a fundamental skill that can significantly impact professional relationships, team dynamics, and overall organizational success.

## Introduction To Empathy In The Workplace

Empathy is the ability to understand and share the feelings of another. In professional settings, it involves recognizing and responding appropriately to the emotions, experiences, and perspectives of colleagues, superiors, subordinates, and clients.

There are three main types of empathy:

1. **Cognitive Empathy**: The ability to understand how a

person might think or feel in a given situation. It's about perspective-taking.
2. **Emotional Empathy**: The capacity to actually feel what another person is feeling.
3. **Compassionate Empathy**: Combining understanding with action - not just understanding a person's predicament and feeling with them, but being spontaneously moved to help, if needed.

In the workplace, a balance of all three types is often necessary, with an emphasis on cognitive and compassionate empathy.

## The Neuroscience Of Empathy

Understanding the brain science behind empathy can help us appreciate its innate human quality and its potential for development.

**Mirror Neurons**: These specialized brain cells fire both when we perform an action and when we observe someone else performing the same action. They play a crucial role in our ability to understand and empathize with others' actions and emotions.

**The Empathy Circuit**: Several brain regions work together to enable empathy, including:

- The anterior insula, involved in self-awareness and emotional experiences
- The anterior cingulate cortex, which plays a role in emotional regulation
- The medial prefrontal cortex, important for perspective-taking and understanding others' mental states

This neural basis suggests that while we may have natural tendencies towards empathy, it's also a skill that can be developed and strengthened over time.

## The Benefits Of Empathy In The Workplace

Empathy in professional environments can lead to numerous positive outcomes:

1. **Improved Team Collaboration**: Empathetic team members are better at understanding each other's perspectives, leading to smoother collaboration and fewer conflicts.
2. **Enhanced Leadership Effectiveness**: Leaders who demonstrate empathy are often more successful at motivating and engaging their teams.
3. **Better Customer Relations**: Understanding and anticipating customer needs leads to improved service and increased customer loyalty.
4. **Increased Innovation**: Empathy can drive innovation by helping us understand user needs and pain points more deeply.
5. **Higher Employee Engagement**: Employees who feel understood and valued tend to be more engaged and committed to their work.

## Barriers To Empathy In Professional Environments

Despite its benefits, several factors can hinder empathy in the workplace:

1. **Time Pressure and Stress**: When we're overwhelmed, it's harder to take the time to understand others' perspectives.
2. **Power Dynamics**: Hierarchical structures can sometimes create emotional distance between levels.
3. **Cultural Differences**: Misunderstandings due to cultural variances can impede empathy.
4. **Digital Communication**: The lack of face-to-face

interaction in digital environments can make empathy more challenging.
5. **Competitive Environments**: Some workplace cultures may inadvertently discourage empathy in favor of individual achievement.

## Developing Empathy Skills

Empathy is a skill that can be cultivated. Here are some strategies:

1. **Active Listening**: Focus entirely on the speaker, avoiding interruptions and truly trying to understand their perspective.
2. **Perspective-Taking Exercises**: Regularly challenge yourself to see situations from others' viewpoints.
3. **Cultivating Curiosity**: Approach interactions with genuine interest in learning about others.
4. **Non-Judgmental Observation**: Practice observing others' emotions and behaviors without immediately judging them.
5. **Empathy Mapping**: A visual tool used to gain insights about a user's needs and pain points.

## Empathy In Diverse And Inclusive Workplaces

In today's global work environment, empathy plays a crucial role in fostering inclusivity:

1. **Understanding Different Experiences**: Recognize that colleagues from diverse backgrounds may have vastly different life experiences that shape their perspectives.
2. **Addressing Unconscious Biases**: Be aware of your own biases and how they might affect your empathy towards certain groups.
3. **Creating an Empathetic Culture**: Encourage sharing of diverse viewpoints and experiences to build mutual

understanding.

## Empathy In Leadership

Empathetic leadership can transform team dynamics:

1. **Characteristics of Empathetic Leaders**:
   - They listen more than they speak
   - They seek to understand before making judgments
   - They are approachable and create psychologically safe environments
2. **Using Empathy to Motivate**: Understanding team members' individual motivations and concerns allows leaders to inspire more effectively.
3. **Balancing Empathy and Decision-Making**: While empathy is crucial, leaders must also make tough decisions. The key is to make these decisions with a full understanding of their impact on others.

## Empathy In Conflict Resolution

Empathy can be a powerful tool in managing workplace conflicts:

1. **De-escalation**: Showing empathy can help calm heated situations by demonstrating that all parties feel heard.
2. **Finding Win-Win Solutions**: Understanding all perspectives can lead to solutions that benefit everyone involved.
3. **Empathetic Mediation**: When mediating conflicts, use empathy to help each party understand the other's viewpoint.

## Empathy In Customer Relations

For customer-facing roles, empathy is essential:

1. **Understanding Customer Needs**: Use empathy to anticipate and address customer needs proactively.
2. **Handling Difficult Situations**: Empathy can help diffuse tension when dealing with upset customers.
3. **Building Long-Term Relationships**: Customers who feel understood are more likely to remain loyal to a brand or service.

## The Limits Of Empathy: Avoiding Empathy Burnout

While empathy is valuable, it's important to maintain boundaries to avoid burnout:

1. **Recognizing Empathy Fatigue**: Signs include emotional exhaustion, reduced performance, and compassion fatigue.
2. **Setting Healthy Boundaries**: It's okay (and necessary) to sometimes prioritize your own needs.
3. **Self-Care Strategies**: Regular self-care practices can help maintain your capacity for empathy.

## Measuring And Assessing Empathy In The Workplace

While empathy can be challenging to quantify, several methods can help:

1. **Empathy Quotient Assessments**: Standardized tests that measure an individual's empathy levels.
2. **360-Degree Feedback**: Gathering input from colleagues, subordinates, and superiors about empathetic behaviors.
3. **Empathy-Related KPIs**: Metrics like customer satisfaction scores or team cohesion ratings can

indirectly reflect empathy levels.

## Technology And Empathy

In our increasingly digital workplaces, maintaining empathy presents unique challenges:

1. **Digital Communication Challenges**: Lack of non-verbal cues can make empathetic communication more difficult.
2. **Tools for Virtual Empathy**: Video conferencing, emojis, and GIFs can help convey emotion in digital communication.
3. **AI and Empathy**: Emerging AI technologies are being developed to recognize and respond to human emotions, potentially supporting empathy in digital environments.

## Teaching And Promoting Empathy In Organizations

Organizations can actively foster empathy:

1. **Empathy Training Programs**: Workshops and courses can help employees develop empathy skills.
2. **Incorporating Empathy into Company Values**: Make empathy an explicit part of your organizational culture.
3. **Rewarding Empathetic Behavior**: Recognize and reward employees who demonstrate strong empathy skills.

## Practical Exercises For Enhancing Empathy

1. **Empathy Mapping**: Create visual representations of others' thoughts, feelings, and motivations.
2. **Role-Playing**: Act out scenarios from different

perspectives to build understanding.
3. **"A Day in Their Shoes"**: Spend a day doing someone else's job to gain insight into their challenges and perspectives.

## Conclusion: Integrating Empathy Into Your Professional Identity

Developing empathy is an ongoing process that requires consistent effort and practice. By making empathy a core part of your professional identity, you can enhance your relationships, improve your effectiveness, and contribute to a more positive and productive work environment.

Remember, empathy doesn't mean always agreeing with others or compromising your own needs. Rather, it's about creating a foundation of understanding from which more effective communication, collaboration, and problem-solving can emerge.

In our next chapter, we'll explore how to leverage empathy and the other EI skills we've discussed to navigate complex workplace dynamics and build strong professional relationships.

# CHAPTER 5

# Social Skills: Navigating Complex Workplace Dynamics

As we've journeyed through the components of Emotional Intelligence (EI), we've explored self-awareness, self-regulation, and empathy. Now, we turn our attention to the culmination of these skills: social skills. In the workplace, social skills are the outward manifestation of emotional intelligence, allowing us to navigate complex interpersonal dynamics effectively.

## Introduction To Social Skills In The Professional Context

Social skills in the context of emotional intelligence refer to our ability to interact effectively with others, build relationships, and navigate social environments. In the professional world, these skills are crucial for collaboration, leadership, and career advancement.

The link between social skills and career success is well-established. A study by Harvard University, the Carnegie Foundation, and Stanford Research Center found that 85% of job success comes from having well-developed soft skills and people skills, while only 15% comes from technical skills and knowledge.

## Key Components Of Social Skills In The Workplace

1. **Effective Communication**: This includes both verbal and non-verbal communication. It's about expressing ideas clearly and listening actively to others.
2. **Active Listening**: The ability to fully concentrate, understand, respond, and remember what is being said.
3. **Relationship Building**: Creating and maintaining positive professional relationships with colleagues, superiors, and clients.
4. **Networking**: The art of creating and utilizing professional connections for mutual benefit.
5. **Collaboration and Teamwork**: Working effectively with others towards common goals.
6. **Conflict Resolution**: The ability to address and resolve disagreements constructively.
7. **Persuasion and Influence**: The capacity to win others over to your point of view or course of action.
8. **Adaptability and Flexibility**: The ability to adjust your approach based on different people and situations.

## The Role Of Social Skills In Different Professional Situations

### Meetings and Presentations

In these settings, social skills help you read the room, engage your audience, and communicate your ideas effectively. They also enable you to handle questions and objections gracefully.

## One-on-One Interactions

Whether it's with a colleague, superior, or direct report, strong social skills allow for clear communication, mutual understanding, and productive outcomes.

## Team Projects

Social skills are crucial for fostering collaboration, managing group dynamics, and ensuring everyone's contributions are valued and utilized.

## Networking Events

The ability to strike up conversations, make memorable impressions, and follow up effectively can significantly expand your professional opportunities.

## Performance Reviews

Social skills help in delivering feedback constructively and receiving feedback openly, turning these potentially stressful interactions into opportunities for growth.

## Negotiations

Whether you're negotiating a salary, a contract, or a project timeline, social skills help you understand the other party's position and find mutually beneficial solutions.

## Cultural Intelligence And Social Skills

In our increasingly globalized business world, cultural intelligence is a crucial aspect of social skills:

1. **Navigating Cultural Differences**: Understanding and respecting different communication styles, business etiquette, and social norms across cultures.

2. **Building Rapport Across Cultural Boundaries**: Finding common ground and establishing trust with colleagues and clients from diverse backgrounds.
3. **Avoiding Cultural Faux Pas**: Being aware of and sensitive to cultural taboos and expectations in international business settings.

## Digital Social Skills

The rise of remote work and digital communication has made digital social skills increasingly important:

1. **Email and Instant Messaging Etiquette**: Understanding the appropriate tone, response time, and format for different types of digital communication.
2. **Virtual Meeting Participation**: Engaging effectively in video conferences, managing your on-screen presence, and navigating the nuances of virtual team dynamics.
3. **Building Relationships Remotely**: Creating connections and maintaining team cohesion in distributed work environments.
4. **Social Media Professionalism**: Managing your professional online presence and engaging appropriately on professional social networks.

## Developing Charisma And Executive Presence

Charisma and executive presence can significantly enhance your social effectiveness in the workplace:

1. **Components of Charisma**: These include warmth, competence, and presence. Charismatic individuals make others feel valued and inspired.
2. **Enhancing Personal Presence**: This involves body language, vocal tone, and the ability to command attention in a room.

3. **Balancing Authority with Approachability**: Effective leaders are both respected and liked, striking a balance between assertiveness and warmth.

## The Art Of Giving And Receiving Feedback

Feedback is a crucial aspect of workplace communication:

1. **Constructive Criticism Techniques**: Focus on specific behaviors, not personality. Use the "sandwich" method: positive-improvement-positive.
2. **Accepting Feedback Gracefully**: Listen without becoming defensive, ask for clarification, and express appreciation for the feedback.
3. **Creating a Feedback Culture**: Encourage regular, informal feedback in addition to formal reviews.

## Navigating Office Politics

Understanding and navigating office politics is an often-overlooked but crucial social skill:

1. **Understanding Power Dynamics**: Recognize both formal and informal power structures in your organization.
2. **Building Alliances**: Cultivate positive relationships across different departments and levels of the organization.
3. **Ethical Considerations**: Navigate office politics with integrity, avoiding manipulation or stepping on others to get ahead.

## Conflict Management And Resolution

Conflict is inevitable in any workplace. Strong social skills help in managing and resolving conflicts effectively:

1. **Identifying Conflict Sources**: Understanding the root causes of disagreements, whether they're task-based, relationship-based, or due to miscommunication.
2. **De-escalation Strategies**: Use active listening, empathy, and calm communication to reduce tensions.
3. **Mediation Techniques**: When mediating conflicts between others, remain neutral, focus on interests rather than positions, and guide parties towards mutually acceptable solutions.
4. **Turning Conflicts into Opportunities**: View conflicts as chances to improve processes, relationships, and understanding.

## Leadership And Social Skills

Leadership effectiveness is deeply tied to social skills:

1. **Motivating and Inspiring Teams**: Use your social skills to understand what drives your team members and inspire them towards common goals.
2. **Creating a Positive Work Environment**: Foster a culture of open communication, mutual respect, and collaboration.
3. **Adapting Leadership Style**: Use your social awareness to adjust your leadership approach based on the needs of different team members and situations.

## Emotional Contagion In The Workplace

Emotions can spread through a workplace, influencing the overall atmosphere:

1. **Understanding Emotional Contagion**: Recognize how your emotions and those of others can affect the group

dynamic.
2. **Positive Emotional Contagion**: Use your own positive emotions to uplift team morale and create a more positive work environment.
3. **Mitigating Negative Emotions**: Be aware of and address sources of negative emotions before they spread through the team.

## Building And Maintaining Professional Networks

Networking is a crucial social skill for career advancement:

1. **Effective Networking Strategies**: Focus on giving as well as receiving. Show genuine interest in others and look for ways to add value.
2. **Nurturing Long-term Relationships**: Regular check-ins, offering help, and sharing relevant information can keep your network strong over time.
3. **Leveraging Networks**: Use your network ethically for job opportunities, advice, and collaboration.

## Assertiveness In The Workplace

Being assertive allows you to stand up for your rights while respecting others:

1. **Balancing Assertiveness with Respect**: Express your needs and opinions clearly and confidently, while also being considerate of others.
2. **Saying 'No' Professionally**: Learn to decline requests that don't align with your priorities or capacity, while maintaining positive relationships.
3. **Standing Up for Your Ideas**: Present your thoughts with confidence, backed by clear reasoning and openness to discussion.

## Dealing With Difficult Personalities

Every workplace has challenging personalities. Strong social skills can help you navigate these situations:

1. **Strategies for Challenging Colleagues**: Maintain professionalism, set clear boundaries, and focus on work-related issues rather than personal conflicts.
2. **Managing Up**: When dealing with difficult superiors, focus on understanding their priorities, communicating clearly, and finding ways to make their job easier.
3. **Maintaining Professionalism**: Even in trying circumstances, keep your composure and focus on productive solutions.

## The Impact Of Social Skills On Organizational Culture

Individual social skills collectively shape the overall workplace atmosphere:

1. **Open Communication**: When individuals communicate effectively, it fosters a culture of transparency and trust.
2. **Collaboration**: Strong social skills promote a more collaborative and innovative organizational culture.
3. **Positive Work Environment**: Individuals with good social skills contribute to a more positive, supportive work atmosphere.

## Measuring And Improving Social Skills

Like other aspects of emotional intelligence, social skills can be assessed and improved:

1. **Self-assessment Tools**: Use standardized tests or reflective exercises to gauge your social skills.
2. **Seeking Feedback**: Ask colleagues and mentors for honest feedback about your interpersonal effectiveness.
3. **Professional Development**: Seek out workshops, courses, or coaching to enhance specific social skills.

## Practical Exercises For Enhancing Social Skills

1. **Role-playing Scenarios**: Practice difficult conversations or presentations with a trusted colleague.
2. **Communication Style Assessments**: Use tools like DISC or Myers-Briggs to understand your communication style and how to adapt it.
3. **Networking Challenge**: Set a goal to make a new professional connection each week and follow up to nurture the relationship.

## Conclusion: Integrating Advanced Social Skills Into Your Professional Life

Developing strong social skills is an ongoing process that requires consistent effort and practice. By honing these skills, you can navigate complex workplace dynamics more effectively, build stronger professional relationships, and advance your career.

Remember, the goal isn't to manipulate others, but to create genuine connections and mutually beneficial interactions. As you continue to develop your emotional intelligence, you'll find that strong social skills not only benefit you professionally but also contribute to a more positive and productive work environment for everyone.

In our next chapter, we'll explore how to apply all the emotional intelligence skills we've discussed in specific workplace scenarios, from giving presentations to handling difficult conversations.

# CHAPTER 6

# Active Listening: The Art of Truly Hearing Your Colleagues

As we continue our exploration of Emotional Intelligence in the workplace, we turn our attention to a fundamental yet often overlooked skill: active listening. This chapter will delve into the art of truly hearing your colleagues, a skill that underpins effective communication, strong relationships, and successful leadership.

## Introduction To Active Listening

Active listening is more than just hearing words; it's the practice of fully concentrating, understanding, responding, and then remembering what is being said. In the workplace, active listening is crucial for clear communication, building trust, and fostering a positive work environment.

The difference between hearing and listening is significant:

- Hearing is a passive, physical act of perceiving sound.

- Listening is an active, mental process of interpreting and understanding the meaning behind those sounds.

## The Components Of Active Listening

1. **Paying Attention**: Give the speaker your undivided attention and acknowledge the message.
2. **Withholding Judgment**: Be open to new ideas, perspectives, and possibilities.
3. **Reflecting**: Mirror the speaker's information and emotions by periodically paraphrasing key points.
4. **Clarifying**: Ask questions to ensure you understand the intended message.
5. **Summarizing**: Restate key themes to confirm understanding.
6. **Sharing**: Offer your own ideas, feelings, and suggestions, without dominating the conversation.

## The Neuroscience Of Listening

Understanding how our brain processes auditory information can help us become better listeners:

- The auditory cortex processes sound inputs.
- The Wernicke's area helps in understanding spoken language.
- The prefrontal cortex is involved in focusing attention and processing the meaning of the message.
- The hippocampus plays a crucial role in moving information from short-term to long-term memory.

Effective listening requires engaging multiple brain regions simultaneously, which is why it can be mentally demanding but also incredibly rewarding.

## Barriers To Effective Listening In The Workplace

Several factors can impede our ability to listen effectively:

1. **Distractions and Multitasking**: The modern workplace is full of interruptions that can divert our attention.
2. **Preconceived Notions and Biases**: Our own beliefs and prejudices can color how we interpret messages.
3. **Emotional Reactions**: Strong emotions can interfere with our ability to listen objectively.
4. **Information Overload**: In our data-rich world, it's easy to become overwhelmed with information.
5. **Cultural and Language Differences**: Miscommunications can arise from different cultural norms or language barriers.

## Non-Verbal Aspects Of Active Listening

Active listening isn't just about what you hear; it's also about what you express non-verbally:

1. **Body Language**: Lean slightly forward, maintain an open posture, and nod occasionally to show engagement.
2. **Facial Expressions**: Your face should reflect attentiveness and interest.
3. **Eye Contact**: Maintain appropriate eye contact to signal focus and respect.
4. **Posture and Positioning**: Face the speaker and minimize physical barriers between you.

## Techniques For Improving Active Listening Skills

1. **Mindfulness and Focused Attention Exercises**: Practice being present in the moment and focusing your attention.
2. **Paraphrasing and Repeating Back**: Restate what you've

heard in your own words to confirm understanding.
3. **Asking Open-ended Questions**: Encourage the speaker to elaborate and provide more information.
4. **Using Silence Effectively**: Don't rush to fill pauses; allow the speaker time to gather thoughts.

## Active Listening In Different Workplace Scenarios

### One-on-One Conversations

Give your full attention, maintain eye contact, and use verbal and non-verbal cues to show you're engaged.

### Team Meetings

Practice inclusive listening, ensuring all voices are heard and understood.

### Presentations and Speeches

Focus on the speaker, take notes if necessary, and prepare thoughtful questions.

### Customer Interactions

Listen for both explicit and implicit needs, showing genuine interest in the customer's perspective.

### Conflict Resolution

Use active listening to understand all sides of the issue, helping to find common ground and solutions.

## The Role Of Active Listening In Leadership

Leaders who are skilled active listeners can:

- Build trust and respect among team members
- Make more informed decisions based on a fuller

understanding of situations
- Create an environment where employees feel valued and heard

To create a culture of listening:
- Model good listening behavior
- Encourage open communication
- Recognize and reward effective listening in the organization

## Active Listening In Virtual Environments

The rise of remote work presents unique challenges for active listening:

1. **Minimize Distractions**: Create a dedicated workspace and use noise-cancelling headphones if necessary.
2. **Utilize Video**: When possible, use video conferencing to pick up on non-verbal cues.
3. **Practice 'Digital Body Language'**: Use appropriate reactions, nods, and verbal affirmations to show engagement.
4. **Follow Up in Writing**: Summarize key points after virtual meetings to ensure clear understanding.

## Empathetic Listening

Empathetic listening goes beyond understanding words to grasp emotions and intentions:

1. **Listen for Feelings**: Pay attention to tone of voice, pace, and emotional undertones.
2. **Validate Emotions**: Acknowledge the speaker's feelings without necessarily agreeing with their perspective.
3. **Avoid Problem-Solving Too Quickly**: Sometimes, people just need to be heard rather than given solutions.

## Listening Across Cultures

In diverse workplaces, be aware of cultural differences in communication:

1. **Direct vs. Indirect Communication**: Some cultures value direct speech, while others prefer more subtle communication.
2. **Silence and Pauses**: The meaning and comfort with silence can vary greatly across cultures.
3. **Non-verbal Cues**: Gestures, eye contact, and personal space norms differ across cultures.

Adapt your listening style accordingly and always approach cross-cultural communication with an open and respectful mindset.

## The Connection Between Active Listening And Other Ei Skills

Active listening enhances and is enhanced by other emotional intelligence skills:

- **Self-Awareness**: Understanding your own biases and reactions improves your ability to listen objectively.
- **Self-Regulation**: Managing your own emotions allows you to listen without becoming defensive or reactive.
- **Empathy**: Active listening is a key component of empathy, allowing you to truly understand others' perspectives.
- **Social Skills**: Effective listening is fundamental to building strong relationships and navigating social situations.

## Overcoming Personal Barriers To Listening

Recognize your own listening weaknesses:

- Do you interrupt frequently?
- Do you formulate responses before the speaker has finished?
- Do you let your mind wander to unrelated topics?

Develop strategies to address these habits, such as consciously pausing before responding or taking notes to stay focused.

## The Impact Of Active Listening On Workplace Relationships

Active listening can significantly improve workplace dynamics by:

- Building trust and rapport
- Reducing misunderstandings and conflicts
- Fostering a sense of value and respect among team members
- Encouraging more open and honest communication

## Measuring And Assessing Listening Skills

To improve your listening skills, it's important to assess your current abilities:

1. **Self-Assessment**: Reflect on your listening habits and areas for improvement.
2. **Feedback**: Ask colleagues for honest feedback about your listening skills.
3. **Formal Assessments**: Consider using standardized listening assessment tools.

## The Role Of Listening In Problem-Solving And Decision-Making

Active listening contributes to better problem-solving by:

- Ensuring a full understanding of the issue at hand
- Gathering diverse perspectives and ideas
- Creating an environment where team members feel their input is valued

## Listening In Difficult Conversations

When emotions run high:

- Stay calm and focused
- Listen without interrupting, even if you disagree
- Acknowledge emotions without getting drawn into them
- Use clarifying questions to ensure understanding

## Teaching And Promoting Active Listening In Organizations

Organizations can promote active listening by:

- Offering workshops and training sessions on listening skills
- Incorporating listening effectiveness into performance evaluations
- Recognizing and rewarding good listeners in the organization

## Practical Exercises For Enhancing Listening Skills

1. **The Repeating Exercise**: In pairs, have one person speak for a minute, then have the listener repeat back what they heard.
2. **The Distraction Challenge**: Practice listening while mild distractions are introduced, gradually increasing difficulty.
3. **The Empathy Map**: After a conversation, fill out an empathy map noting what the speaker said, did,

thought, and felt.

## Conclusion: Integrating Active Listening Into Your Daily Professional Life

Developing strong active listening skills is a lifelong journey. It requires consistent practice and a genuine desire to understand others. By committing to improving your listening skills, you can enhance your effectiveness in the workplace, build stronger relationships, and contribute to a more positive and productive work environment.

Remember, the goal of active listening is not just to hear words, but to truly understand the complete message being conveyed. As you continue to develop this skill, you'll likely find that it not only improves your professional interactions but also enriches your personal relationships and overall communication experiences.

In our next chapter, we'll explore how to apply emotional intelligence skills, including active listening, in specific challenging workplace scenarios.

# CHAPTER 7

# Non-Verbal Communication: Reading and Projecting Body Language

In our journey through the landscape of Emotional Intelligence in the workplace, we've explored various aspects of interpersonal communication. Now, we turn our attention to a powerful yet often overlooked dimension: non-verbal communication. This chapter will delve into the art and science of reading and projecting body language in professional settings.

## Introduction To Non-Verbal Communication In The Workplace

Non-verbal communication encompasses all the ways we convey messages without words. It includes facial expressions, gestures, posture, eye contact, and even our use of space. In the workplace, these silent signals can speak volumes, often carrying more weight than our verbal messages.

The importance of non-verbal communication in professional

settings cannot be overstated:
- It can reinforce or contradict what is being said verbally
- It helps in building rapport and trust
- It can convey emotions and attitudes that might be inappropriate to express in words
- It plays a crucial role in how we are perceived by colleagues, superiors, and clients

## The Science Behind Non-Verbal Communication

Understanding the biological basis of non-verbal communication can help us appreciate its significance:

- The brain processes non-verbal cues in the right hemisphere, often more quickly than verbal information processed in the left hemisphere.
- Mirror neurons in our brains fire both when we perform an action and when we observe someone else performing the same action, helping us understand and empathize with others' experiences.
- Many non-verbal behaviors have evolutionary roots, such as widening eyes in fear to take in more visual information about a threat.

## Types Of Non-Verbal Communication

1. **Facial Expressions**: Often the most telling aspect of non-verbal communication. The human face is extremely expressive, capable of conveying countless emotions without saying a word.
2. **Eye Contact**: In many cultures, eye contact is a crucial component of communication, signaling attention, interest, and honesty.
3. **Gestures**: Hand movements can emphasize points, express ideas, or convey emotions. However, the

meaning of gestures can vary significantly across cultures.
4. **Posture and Body Positioning**: How we hold our body can communicate confidence, openness, defensiveness, or engagement.
5. **Proxemics (Use of Space)**: The distance we maintain from others can indicate comfort level, cultural norms, or the nature of the relationship.
6. **Touch**: In professional contexts, touch is usually limited but can include handshakes, pats on the back, or other culturally appropriate forms of contact.
7. **Paralanguage**: This refers to vocal communication that is separate from the actual language spoken, including factors such as tone of voice, loudness, inflection, and pitch.

## Cultural Differences In Non-Verbal Communication

Non-verbal cues can vary dramatically across cultures:

- In some cultures, direct eye contact is seen as respectful, while in others it may be considered challenging or disrespectful.
- Personal space norms differ widely, with some cultures preferring closer physical proximity than others.
- Gestures that are innocuous in one culture may be offensive in another.

In multicultural workplaces, it's crucial to:

- Be aware of these differences
- Avoid making assumptions based on your own cultural norms
- Observe and learn from colleagues' non-verbal behaviors
- When in doubt, ask respectfully about cultural norms

## Reading Non-Verbal Cues In Others

Developing the ability to accurately read non-verbal cues is a valuable skill:

1. **Look for Congruence**: Notice if verbal and non-verbal messages align. Incongruence often signals discomfort or dishonesty.
2. **Observe Clusters**: Single non-verbal cues can be misleading. Look for groups of behaviors that point to the same message.
3. **Consider Context**: Interpret behaviors within the situation. Crossed arms might indicate defensiveness, or simply that the room is cold.
4. **Baseline Behavior**: Understand an individual's typical behavior to better recognize deviations that might signal something significant.

Common non-verbal indicators in the workplace:

- Engagement: Leaning forward, maintaining eye contact, nodding
- Disinterest: Checking the time, fidgeting, avoiding eye contact
- Agreement: Nodding, open posture, mirroring the speaker's body language
- Disagreement: Furrowed brow, tight lips, shaking head slightly

## Projecting Confident And Professional Body Language

How you carry yourself can significantly impact how you're perceived:

1. **Posture**: Stand or sit up straight with shoulders back to project confidence.
2. **Eye Contact**: Maintain appropriate eye contact to convey interest and honesty.

3. **Handshakes**: A firm (but not crushing) handshake often makes a good first impression in many Western business contexts.
4. **Facial Expressions**: Be aware of your facial expressions, aiming for a pleasant, attentive look.
5. **Gestures**: Use natural, open hand gestures to emphasize points and appear more engaging.
6. **Personal Space**: Respect others' personal space while maintaining a professional distance.

## Non-Verbal Communication In Specific Workplace Scenarios

### Job Interviews

- Project confidence through good posture and a firm handshake
- Maintain appropriate eye contact with all interviewers
- Use engaged body language (leaning slightly forward, nodding) to show interest

### Presentations and Public Speaking

- Use deliberate gestures to emphasize key points
- Move purposefully to engage different parts of the audience
- Maintain an open posture to appear confident and approachable

### Negotiations

- Control your facial expressions to avoid revealing too much
- Use mirroring techniques to build rapport
- Be aware of power poses and when to use them

### Conflict Resolution

- Maintain a calm, open posture to de-escalate tensions
- Use a measured tone of voice

- Demonstrate active listening through nodding and appropriate facial expressions

## Non-Verbal Communication In Virtual Environments

The rise of remote work presents unique challenges for non-verbal communication:

1. **Framing**: Ensure your camera is at eye level and you're well-framed in the shot.
2. **Eye Contact**: Look into the camera when speaking to simulate eye contact.
3. **Background**: Be mindful of what's visible behind you and how it might be perceived.
4. **Gestures**: Use slightly exaggerated gestures to compensate for the limitations of video.
5. **Facial Expressions**: Be more expressive than you might be in person to convey engagement.

## The Interplay Between Verbal And Non-Verbal Communication

For effective communication:

- Ensure your non-verbal cues align with your verbal message
- Use non-verbal cues to emphasize and reinforce your words
- Be aware of contradictions between what you're saying and how you're saying it

## Non-Verbal Communication And Emotional Intelligence

Strong emotional intelligence enhances your ability to read and project body language:

- Self-awareness helps you understand your own non-verbal tells
- Self-regulation allows you to control your non-verbal signals
- Empathy improves your ability to accurately interpret others' non-verbal cues
- Social skills help you adapt your non-verbal communication to different situations

## Improving Your Non-Verbal Communication Skills

1. **Self-Assessment**: Record yourself in various professional interactions and analyze your body language.
2. **Seek Feedback**: Ask trusted colleagues for honest feedback about your non-verbal communication style.
3. **Practice Mindfulness**: Being present in the moment can help you be more aware of both your own and others' non-verbal cues.
4. **Role-Playing Exercises**: Practice different scenarios with a partner, focusing on non-verbal elements.

## Managing Non-Verbal Communication In High-Stress Situations

Under stress, our non-verbal cues can betray us. To maintain composure:

- Practice deep breathing to stay calm
- Be aware of your stress tells (e.g., fidgeting, avoiding eye contact) and consciously control them
- Use power poses before stressful situations to boost confidence

## The Role Of Clothing And Appearance

While not strictly "body language," appearance is a form of non-verbal communication:

- Dress appropriately for your workplace culture and role
- Be aware of the messages your clothing choices might send
- Remember that grooming and personal hygiene also communicate professionalism

## Conclusion: Integrating Non-Verbal Communication Awareness Into Your Professional Life

Developing strong non-verbal communication skills is an ongoing process. By becoming more aware of the non-verbal cues you project and improving your ability to read others' body language, you can significantly enhance your overall communication effectiveness in the workplace.

Remember, the goal is not to completely control every non-verbal signal you send – that would likely come across as unnatural or insincere. Instead, aim for greater awareness and intentionality in your non-verbal communication, aligning it with your words and intentions to create more impactful, authentic interactions in your professional life.

In our next chapter, we'll explore how to apply all the emotional intelligence skills we've discussed, including non-verbal communication, in handling conflicts and difficult conversations in the workplace.

# CHAPTER 8

# Conflict Resolution: Using EI to Navigate Disagreements

As we continue our exploration of Emotional Intelligence in the workplace, we now turn our attention to one of the most challenging aspects of professional life: conflict resolution. In this chapter, we'll examine how the EI skills we've discussed in previous chapters can be applied to navigate disagreements effectively and turn conflicts into opportunities for growth and innovation.

## Introduction To Conflict In The Workplace

Conflict is an inevitable part of human interaction, and the workplace is no exception. Conflicts can arise from various sources:

- Differences in opinions, values, or beliefs
- Competition for resources or recognition
- Miscommunication or misunderstandings
- Personality clashes
- Organizational changes or uncertainties

While often viewed negatively, conflict isn't inherently bad. When managed effectively, it can lead to better decisions, increased creativity, and stronger relationships. The key lies in how we approach and resolve these disagreements, which is where emotional intelligence plays a crucial role.

## Understanding The Nature Of Conflict

To effectively manage conflicts, it's important to understand their nature:

1. **Cognitive vs. Emotional Conflicts**:
   - Cognitive conflicts focus on task-related disagreements and can often be productive.
   - Emotional conflicts involve personal friction and are typically more challenging to resolve.
2. **Constructive vs. Destructive Conflicts**:
   - Constructive conflicts lead to positive outcomes, such as improved ideas or processes.
   - Destructive conflicts harm relationships and hinder productivity.
3. **Common Sources of Workplace Conflicts**:
   - Unclear job roles or responsibilities
   - Differences in work styles or approaches
   - Limited resources or high-stress environments
   - Poor communication or lack of information
   - Conflicting goals or priorities

## The Impact Of Unresolved Conflicts

Left unaddressed, conflicts can have serious negative consequences:

- Decreased productivity and morale
- Increased stress and anxiety among team members

- Breakdown in communication and collaboration
- Higher employee turnover
- Negative impact on organizational culture and reputation

## Self-Awareness In Conflict Situations

The first step in effective conflict resolution is self-awareness:

1. **Recognizing Your Emotional Triggers**:
   - Identify what situations or behaviors tend to provoke strong emotional reactions in you.
   - Understanding your triggers helps you prepare for and manage your responses more effectively.
2. **Understanding Your Conflict Management Style**:
   - Are you naturally inclined to compete, accommodate, avoid, compromise, or collaborate?
   - Each style has its strengths and weaknesses; the key is knowing when to use which approach.
3. **Identifying Your Biases and Preconceptions**:
   - We all have biases that can affect how we perceive and respond to conflicts.
   - Recognizing these biases allows us to approach conflicts more objectively.

## Self-Regulation Strategies For Managing Emotions During Conflicts

Maintaining emotional control is crucial for effective conflict resolution:

1. **Techniques for Staying Calm Under Pressure**:
   - Practice deep breathing exercises
   - Use mental imagery to visualize a calm, positive outcome
   - Take a brief pause or time-out if emotions are running high

2. **Managing Anger and Frustration Constructively**:
   - Recognize anger as a signal, not a solution
   - Express feelings assertively, not aggressively
   - Focus on the issue at hand, not personal attacks
3. **Maintaining Professionalism**:
   - Remember that your behavior during conflicts can impact your professional reputation
   - Strive to be the calm in the storm, setting an example for others

## Empathy In Conflict Resolution

Empathy is a powerful tool for de-escalating conflicts and finding mutually beneficial solutions:

1. **Seeing the Conflict from All Perspectives**:
   - Make a conscious effort to understand the other person's point of view
   - Ask yourself: "What might be driving their behavior or position?"
2. **Understanding Underlying Needs and Motivations**:
   - Often, conflicts arise from unmet needs or fears
   - Try to identify what each party truly needs to feel satisfied
3. **Building Rapport Even in Disagreement**:
   - Find common ground where possible
   - Acknowledge the other person's feelings and perspective, even if you disagree

## Active Listening Skills For Conflict Resolution

Effective listening is crucial for understanding the root of conflicts and finding solutions:

1. **Techniques for Truly Hearing All Sides**:
   - Give your full attention to the speaker

- Avoid interrupting or planning your response while others are speaking
2. **Asking Clarifying Questions**:
- Use open-ended questions to gather more information
- Seek to understand, not to prove a point
3. **Paraphrasing and Summarizing**:
- Reflect back what you've heard to ensure understanding
- This shows you're listening and helps clarify any misunderstandings

## Effective Communication Strategies In Conflicts

How you communicate during conflicts can significantly impact the outcome:

1. **Using "I" Statements**:
- Express your feelings and needs without blaming or accusing
- For example, "I feel frustrated when deadlines are missed" instead of "You always miss deadlines"
2. **Framing Issues Constructively**:
- Focus on the problem, not the person
- Present issues as shared challenges to be solved together
3. **Avoiding Blame and Accusatory Language**:
- Stick to observable facts rather than judgments or assumptions
- Use neutral language to describe situations

## Non-Verbal Communication In Conflict Situations

Remember that your body language speaks volumes:

1. **Reading Body Language Cues**:
- Look for signs of discomfort, defensiveness, or openness in others
- Be aware that stress can make body language more

difficult to read accurately
2. **Managing Your Own Non-Verbal Signals**:
   - Maintain an open posture
   - Use a calm, measured tone of voice
   - Make appropriate eye contact to show engagement and respect
3. **Creating a Non-Threatening Physical Environment**:
   - Choose neutral locations for difficult conversations
   - Arrange seating to promote equality and openness

## Conflict Resolution Models And Frameworks

Several models can guide your approach to conflict resolution:

1. **The Thomas-Kilmann Conflict Mode Instrument**:
   - Identifies five conflict-handling modes: Competing, Collaborating, Compromising, Avoiding, and Accommodating
   - Helps you understand your default style and when to use different approaches
2. **Interest-Based Relational Approach**:
   - Emphasizes maintaining relationships while achieving a mutually beneficial outcome
   - Focuses on interests (why you want something) rather than positions (what you say you want)
3. **The GROW Model for Conflict Resolution**:
   - Goal: Clearly define the desired outcome
   - Reality: Assess the current situation
   - Options: Explore possible solutions
   - Will: Determine the way forward and commit to action

## Negotiation Skills For Win-Win Solutions

Effective negotiation is key to resolving conflicts positively:

1. **Identifying Common Ground**:

- Look for shared interests or goals
- Use these as a foundation for building agreement
2. **Brainstorming Creative Solutions**:
- Encourage thinking outside the box
- Generate multiple options before evaluating them
3. **Techniques for Overcoming Deadlocks**:
- Take breaks to allow emotions to cool and gain fresh perspective
- Consider bringing in a neutral third party to mediate
- Look for small agreements to build momentum

## Mediating Conflicts Between Team Members

As a leader or colleague, you may need to mediate conflicts:

1. **Steps for Effective Mediation**:
- Establish ground rules for the discussion
- Allow each party to share their perspective uninterrupted
- Guide the conversation towards finding a mutually acceptable solution
2. **Remaining Neutral and Objective**:
- Avoid taking sides or showing favoritism
- Focus on facilitating a resolution, not judging who's right or wrong
3. **Guiding Parties Towards Their Own Solutions**:
- Empower the conflicting parties to generate and agree on solutions
- This increases buy-in and the likelihood of a lasting resolution

## Dealing With Difficult Personalities In Conflicts

Some conflicts are exacerbated by challenging personality types:

1. **Strategies for Managing Aggressive Behavior**:

- Stay calm and don't respond with aggression
- Set clear boundaries about acceptable behavior
- Use assertive communication to address the issue directly
2. **Handling Passive-Aggressive Responses**:
- Address the behavior specifically, not the person
- Encourage open, direct communication
- Don't engage in reading between the lines; ask for clarification
3. **Addressing Chronic Complainers Constructively**:
- Listen actively to identify any valid concerns
- Ask for specific, actionable solutions
- Set limits on time spent discussing complaints

## Cultural Considerations In Conflict Resolution

In diverse workplaces, cultural differences can impact conflict resolution:

1. **Understanding Cultural Differences in Conflict Perception**:
- Some cultures view open conflict as normal, while others prioritize harmony
- Be aware of different communication styles (direct vs. indirect)
2. **Adapting Resolution Strategies for Diverse Teams**:
- Be flexible in your approach to accommodate different cultural norms
- When in doubt, ask about preferred ways of addressing disagreements
3. **Avoiding Cultural Misunderstandings**:
- Don't make assumptions based on stereotypes
- Seek to understand the cultural context behind behaviors or reactions

## Conflict Resolution In Remote And Virtual Teams

Remote work presents unique challenges for conflict resolution:

1. **Challenges Specific to Digital Communication**:
   - Lack of non-verbal cues can lead to misunderstandings
   - Asynchronous communication can delay resolution
2. **Techniques for Managing Conflicts in Virtual Meetings**:
   - Use video whenever possible to capture non-verbal cues
   - Establish clear communication protocols for virtual discussions
3. **Building Trust and Understanding in Remote Teams**:
   - Create opportunities for informal virtual interactions
   - Encourage open, frequent communication to prevent misunderstandings

## The Role Of Leadership In Conflict Resolution

Leaders play a crucial role in setting the tone for conflict resolution:

1. **Creating a Culture that Addresses Conflicts Constructively**:
   - Encourage open dialogue and feedback
   - Treat conflicts as opportunities for growth and improvement
2. **When and How Leaders Should Intervene in Conflicts**:
   - Intervene when conflicts affect team performance or morale
   - Provide guidance and resources for resolution, but empower team members to solve their own conflicts when possible
3. **Modeling Effective Conflict Resolution Behaviors**:
   - Demonstrate emotional intelligence in your own

conflict interactions
- Be transparent about how you approach and resolve disagreements

## Post-Conflict Relationship Repair

After a conflict is resolved, it's important to rebuild relationships:

1. **Strategies for Rebuilding Trust:**
   - Follow through on any agreements made during resolution
   - Be consistent in your behavior moving forward
2. **Fostering Forgiveness and Moving Forward:**
   - Acknowledge any harm done and express genuine remorse if necessary
   - Focus on future positive interactions rather than dwelling on past conflicts
3. **Learning from Conflicts to Prevent Future Issues:**
   - Reflect on what led to the conflict and how it was resolved
   - Implement changes to address root causes of recurring conflicts

## Conflict As An Opportunity For Growth And Innovation

Reframe conflicts as chances for positive change:

1. **Using Disagreements to Drive Creativity and Improvement:**
   - Encourage diverse perspectives and constructive debate
   - Look for innovative solutions that emerge from differing viewpoints
2. **Building Resilience Through Conflict Resolution:**
   - Each successfully navigated conflict builds confidence

          and skills
        o Celebrate the growth and learning that comes from resolving disagreements

## Conclusion: Integrating Ei-Based Conflict Resolution Into Your Professional Life

Developing strong conflict resolution skills based on emotional intelligence is an ongoing process. By applying the principles and strategies outlined in this chapter, you can transform conflicts from sources of stress into opportunities for growth, innovation, and stronger professional relationships.

Remember, the goal isn't to eliminate all conflicts, but to navigate them in a way that leads to positive outcomes and strengthens your professional environment. As you continue to develop these skills, you'll likely find that you're not only more effective at resolving conflicts, but also at preventing unnecessary conflicts from arising in the first place.

In our next chapter, we'll explore how to give and receive feedback effectively, another crucial application of emotional intelligence in the workplace.

# CHAPTER 9

# Giving and Receiving Feedback: The EI Approach

In our journey through Emotional Intelligence in the workplace, we've explored various aspects of interpersonal communication and conflict resolution. Now, we turn our attention to a critical component of professional growth and organizational success: the art of giving and receiving feedback. In this chapter, we'll examine how to apply emotional intelligence to make feedback conversations more constructive, meaningful, and impactful.

## Introduction To Feedback In The Workplace

Feedback is a vital tool for personal and professional development. It provides individuals with insights into their performance, behavior, and impact on others, enabling continuous improvement and growth. However, feedback conversations can often be fraught with emotional challenges:

- Fear of giving offense or damaging relationships when providing critical feedback
- Anxiety or defensiveness when receiving feedback, especially

if it's negative
- Difficulty in separating personal feelings from professional critiques

These challenges underscore the importance of applying emotional intelligence to the feedback process.

## The Role Of Emotional Intelligence In Effective Feedback

Emotional intelligence plays a crucial role in both giving and receiving feedback:

1. **Self-awareness**: Understanding your own emotions and biases when giving or receiving feedback.
2. **Self-regulation**: Managing your emotional reactions during feedback conversations.
3. **Empathy**: Understanding the emotional state and perspective of the other person involved in the feedback process.
4. **Social skills**: Communicating feedback in a way that is constructive and well-received.

By leveraging these EI skills, we can transform feedback from a potentially stressful interaction into a powerful tool for growth and collaboration.

## Preparing To Give Feedback

Effective feedback begins with proper preparation:

1. **Set the right mindset**: Approach feedback as a opportunity for mutual growth, not criticism.
2. **Gather specific, observable information**: Base your feedback on concrete examples and data, not hearsay or assumptions.

3. **Choose the appropriate time and place**: Select a private, comfortable setting and ensure you have sufficient uninterrupted time.
4. **Reflect on your intentions**: Ensure your motivation is to help the recipient improve, not to vent frustrations or assert authority.

## The Art Of Giving Constructive Feedback

When delivering feedback, consider the following strategies:

1. **Use the "sandwich" method judiciously**: While starting and ending with positives can soften the impact of criticism, overuse of this technique can feel insincere or formulaic.
2. **Focus on behavior, not personality**: Discuss specific actions or results, not character traits. For example, "The report was submitted after the deadline" rather than "You're unreliable."
3. **Be specific and action-oriented**: Provide clear examples and suggest concrete steps for improvement.
4. **Balance positive and negative feedback**: Recognize strengths and achievements alongside areas for improvement.
5. **Use "I" statements**: Frame feedback from your perspective to avoid sounding accusatory. For example, "I noticed that..." instead of "You always..."

## Active Listening During Feedback Conversations

Effective feedback is a two-way conversation. Practice active listening by:

1. **Giving your full attention**: Minimize distractions and focus entirely on the conversation.
2. **Using verbal and non-verbal cues**: Nod, maintain

appropriate eye contact, and use encouraging phrases to show you're engaged.
3. **Paraphrasing and summarizing**: Reflect back what you've heard to ensure understanding.
4. **Asking clarifying questions**: Seek to understand the recipient's perspective fully.

## Non-Verbal Communication In Feedback Sessions

Pay attention to body language, both yours and the recipient's:

1. **Read the recipient's body language**: Look for signs of discomfort, defensiveness, or openness.
2. **Manage your own non-verbal cues**: Maintain an open posture, use a calm tone of voice, and make appropriate eye contact.
3. **Create a comfortable physical environment**: Arrange seating to promote openness and equality.

## Empathy In Giving Feedback

Empathy is crucial for effective feedback:

1. **Put yourself in the recipient's shoes**: Consider how they might feel receiving this feedback.
2. **Acknowledge emotions**: Recognize and validate the recipient's feelings about the feedback.
3. **Tailor your approach**: Adjust your feedback style based on the individual's personality and preferences.

## Self-Regulation When Giving Difficult Feedback

Delivering challenging feedback can be emotionally taxing. Practice self-regulation by:

1. **Preparing emotionally**: Take time to center yourself

before the conversation.
2. **Monitoring your emotional state**: Be aware of your feelings during the conversation and manage them appropriately.
3. **Taking breaks if needed**: If emotions run high, it's okay to pause and reconvene later.

## Receiving Feedback Gracefully

Receiving feedback effectively is just as important as giving it:

1. **Develop a growth mindset**: View feedback as an opportunity for improvement, not a personal attack.
2. **Manage emotional reactions**: Take a deep breath and stay calm, even if the feedback is unexpected or negative.
3. **Listen actively**: Focus on understanding the feedback fully before responding.
4. **Ask clarifying questions**: Seek specific examples and actionable suggestions.
5. **Express appreciation**: Thank the giver for their input, regardless of whether you agree with all points.

## The Art Of Seeking Feedback

Proactively seeking feedback demonstrates a commitment to growth:

1. **Ask specific questions**: "What's one thing I could improve in my presentations?" is more effective than "How am I doing?"
2. **Create a personal feedback network**: Identify colleagues, mentors, and supervisors who can provide valuable insights.
3. **Set regular feedback check-ins**: Don't wait for formal reviews; seek informal feedback regularly.

## Dealing With Different Types Of Feedback

1. **Positive feedback**: Acknowledge it graciously, but dig deeper to understand specifics of what worked well.
2. **Negative feedback**: Stay open and non-defensive. Focus on learning and improvement opportunities.
3. **Vague feedback**: Ask for specific examples and clarification to make the feedback actionable.

## Cultural Considerations In Feedback

Be aware of cultural differences in feedback styles:

1. **Direct vs. indirect communication**: Some cultures prefer direct feedback, while others favor more subtle approaches.
2. **Individual vs. group focus**: Some cultures emphasize individual performance, while others prioritize group harmony.
3. **Power distance**: In some cultures, giving feedback to superiors may be seen as inappropriate.

Adapt your feedback approach to respect cultural norms while maintaining clarity and constructiveness.

## Feedback In Remote And Virtual Work Environments

Remote work presents unique challenges for feedback:

1. **Use video calls when possible**: This allows for better reading of non-verbal cues.
2. **Be extra clear and specific**: Without in-person context, there's more room for misinterpretation.

3. **Follow up in writing**: Summarize key points in an email to ensure clarity and provide a reference.
4. **Create opportunities for informal feedback**: In the absence of casual office interactions, deliberately create channels for ongoing, informal feedback.

## Creating A Feedback-Rich Organizational Culture

Leaders and organizations can foster a culture that values feedback:

1. **Model good feedback practices**: Leaders should actively seek and thoughtfully give feedback.
2. **Implement regular feedback mechanisms**: This could include pulse surveys, 360-degree reviews, or peer feedback systems.
3. **Recognize and reward feedback behaviors**: Acknowledge those who give and receive feedback effectively.
4. **Provide training**: Offer workshops on giving and receiving feedback using emotional intelligence.

## Feedback And Performance Management

Align feedback with overall performance management:

1. **Connect feedback to goals and expectations**: Ensure feedback relates to established performance criteria.
2. **Use feedback to inform development plans**: Incorporate insights from feedback into personal and professional growth strategies.
3. **Balance ongoing feedback with formal reviews**: While regular informal feedback is crucial, also maintain structured performance review processes.

## Handling Feedback In Difficult Situations

Some feedback situations require extra care:

1. **Addressing recurring issues**: Be clear about consequences and create a specific improvement plan.
2. **Giving feedback to superiors**: Frame feedback in terms of organizational goals and be prepared with specific, constructive suggestions.
3. **Dealing with highly emotional reactions**: Stay calm, acknowledge emotions, and be prepared to continue the conversation at a later time if necessary.

## The Role Of Self-Reflection In The Feedback Process

Use feedback as a tool for enhancing self-awareness:

1. **Reflect on feedback received**: Look for patterns or themes in feedback from various sources.
2. **Compare self-perception with others' perceptions**: Identify any gaps between how you see yourself and how others see you.
3. **Integrate insights into your development plan**: Use feedback to set specific, actionable goals for personal growth.

## Measuring The Effectiveness Of Feedback

Assess the impact of your feedback approach:

1. **Look for behavioral changes**: Observe if feedback leads to noticeable improvements.
2. **Seek meta-feedback**: Ask recipients how they found

your feedback style and if it was helpful.
3. **Track performance metrics**: Where applicable, monitor if feedback correlates with improved performance indicators.

## Common Pitfalls In Giving And Receiving Feedback

Avoid these common mistakes:

1. **Making it personal**: Focus on behaviors and outcomes, not personality traits.
2. **Being too vague**: Provide specific examples and actionable suggestions.
3. **Ignoring emotions**: Acknowledge feelings, both your own and the recipient's.
4. **Failing to follow up**: Check in on progress and offer continued support.

## Conclusion: Integrating Emotionally Intelligent Feedback Into Your Professional Life

Mastering the art of giving and receiving feedback with emotional intelligence is a powerful way to enhance your professional relationships and drive personal and organizational growth. By approaching feedback conversations with self-awareness, empathy, and thoughtfulness, you can transform potentially challenging interactions into valuable opportunities for development and collaboration.

Remember, becoming skilled at feedback is an ongoing process. Continue to practice, seek feedback on your feedback, and refine your approach. As you do so, you'll not only improve your own performance but also contribute to a more open, communicative, and growth-oriented workplace culture.

In our next chapter, we'll explore how to apply emotional intelligence in leadership roles, building on the communication and feedback skills we've discussed to inspire and guide others effectively.

# CHAPTER 10

# Leading with Emotional Intelligence: Inspiring and Motivating Teams

As we culminate our exploration of Emotional Intelligence (EI) in the workplace, we turn our attention to one of its most impactful applications: leadership. In this chapter, we'll examine how emotional intelligence can transform leadership, enabling leaders to inspire, motivate, and guide their teams more effectively.

## Introduction To Emotionally Intelligent Leadership

Emotionally intelligent leadership is the practice of using EI skills to enhance one's ability to lead, influence, and develop others. It involves:

- Understanding and managing one's own emotions
- Recognizing and influencing the emotions of others
- Using emotional awareness to guide decision-making and

behavior

Leaders with high EI are typically more effective because they can:
- Create stronger connections with team members
- Navigate complex interpersonal dynamics
- Make more balanced decisions
- Inspire and motivate others more effectively
- Adapt their leadership style to different situations and individuals

## Self-Awareness In Leadership

Self-awareness is the foundation of emotionally intelligent leadership:

1. **Understanding Your Leadership Style**:
   - Recognize your natural tendencies (e.g., autocratic, democratic, laissez-faire)
   - Understand how your style impacts your team
2. **Recognizing Emotional Triggers and Biases**:
   - Identify situations that provoke strong emotional reactions
   - Be aware of personal biases that might influence decisions
3. **The Impact of a Leader's Emotions**:
   - Understand how your mood affects team morale and performance
   - Practice emotional contagion positively

Exercise: Keep a leadership journal to reflect on your emotions, decisions, and their impacts.

## Self-Regulation For Leaders

Leaders often face high-pressure situations that test their emotional control:

1. **Managing Stress and Pressure**:
   - Develop stress-management techniques (e.g., mindfulness, exercise)
   - Create healthy work-life boundaries
2. **Maintaining Composure**:
   - Practice responding rather than reacting in challenging situations
   - Use techniques like deep breathing or counting to maintain calm
3. **Modeling Emotional Control**:
   - Demonstrate appropriate emotional expression to your team
   - Show how to handle setbacks and failures constructively

Remember, your team will often take cues from your emotional state. Staying composed under pressure sets a powerful example.

# Empathy In Leadership

Empathy allows leaders to connect with and understand their team members:

1. **Understanding Team Members**:
   - Take time to know your team members as individuals
   - Be attentive to their needs, concerns, and motivations
2. **Creating a Supportive Environment**:
   - Foster a culture where people feel heard and valued
   - Encourage open communication and psychological safety
3. **Balancing Empathy with Accountability**:
   - Show understanding while still maintaining high standards
   - Use empathy to deliver constructive feedback more effectively

Exercise: Practice "perspective-taking" by regularly considering situations from your team members' viewpoints.

## Social Skills For Leaders

Strong social skills enable leaders to build relationships and influence others:

1. **Building Relationships**:
   - Cultivate connections across all levels of the organization
   - Show genuine interest in others' ideas and experiences
2. **Networking and Influencing**:
   - Develop your ability to persuade and inspire others
   - Build coalitions to support your initiatives
3. **Communicating Vision**:
   - Articulate your vision in a way that resonates emotionally
   - Use storytelling to make your message more impactful

Remember, effective leadership is as much about relationships as it is about tasks and strategies.

## Motivating And Inspiring Teams

Emotionally intelligent leaders are adept at motivating their teams:

1. **Understanding Motivational Drivers**:
   - Recognize that different people are motivated by different things
   - Take time to understand what drives each team member
2. **Using Emotional Appeals**:
   - Connect organizational goals to personal values and aspirations
   - Use enthusiasm and passion to energize your team
3. **Creating Shared Purpose**:

- Help team members see the bigger picture and their role in it
- Foster a sense of collective mission and shared achievement

Exercise: Have one-on-one conversations with team members to understand their personal goals and how they align with organizational objectives.

## Building Trust And Psychological Safety

Trust is the foundation of high-performing teams:

1. **Importance of Trust**:
   - Understand how trust impacts team performance and innovation
   - Recognize that trust must be earned and can be easily lost
2. **Building Trust**:
   - Be consistent in your words and actions
   - Show vulnerability and admit mistakes
   - Follow through on commitments
3. **Creating Psychological Safety**:
   - Encourage risk-taking and view failures as learning opportunities
   - Foster an environment where all voices are heard and respected

Remember, psychological safety is crucial for creativity, innovation, and honest feedback.

## Emotional Intelligence In Decision-Making

EI can significantly enhance a leader's decision-making:

1. **Balancing Logic and Emotion**:
   - Use both rational analysis and emotional insight

- Consider how decisions will be perceived and felt by others
2. **Considering Emotional Impact:**
- Anticipate how decisions might affect team morale and dynamics
- Prepare strategies to address potential emotional reactions
3. **Navigating Ambiguity:**
- Use emotional cues to guide decisions when data is incomplete
- Stay attuned to your intuition while seeking diverse perspectives

## Leading Through Change And Uncertainty

Change often triggers strong emotions. EI leaders can:

1. **Managing Team Emotions:**
- Acknowledge and validate concerns about change
- Help team members process their emotions constructively
2. **Communicating Effectively:**
- Be transparent about what is known and unknown
- Provide frequent updates to reduce anxiety
3. **Building Resilience:**
- Foster a growth mindset in your team
- Help team members see challenges as opportunities for growth

Exercise: During times of change, schedule regular check-ins with your team to address concerns and provide support.

## Conflict Resolution And Mediation As A Leader

Leaders often need to address conflicts within their teams:

1. **Addressing Team Conflicts**:
   - Intervene early before conflicts escalate
   - Use active listening to understand all perspectives
2. **Mediating Disagreements**:
   - Remain neutral and focus on finding common ground
   - Guide team members towards their own solutions
3. **Using Conflicts for Growth**:
   - Frame conflicts as opportunities for team learning and improvement
   - Encourage constructive debate around ideas

## Giving Feedback And Performance Management

EI is crucial for effective performance management:

1. **Applying EI to Reviews**:
   - Deliver feedback with empathy and clarity
   - Focus on behavior and impact, not personality
2. **Difficult Conversations**:
   - Prepare emotionally for challenging discussions
   - Stay focused on solutions and future improvement
3. **Recognizing EI in Others**:
   - Acknowledge and reward emotionally intelligent behaviors
   - Include EI skills in performance criteria

## Developing Emotional Intelligence In Your Team

Leaders can foster EI throughout their team:

1. **Fostering EI Skills**:
   - Model EI behaviors consistently
   - Provide opportunities for team members to practice EI skills
2. **Creating an EI Culture**:

- Incorporate EI principles into team values and norms
- Recognize and celebrate examples of high EI
3. **Providing Development Opportunities**:
- Offer training and resources on EI
- Encourage mentoring and peer learning around EI skills

## Leading Diverse And Inclusive Teams

EI is essential for effective leadership of diverse teams:

1. **Valuing Different Perspectives**:
- Actively seek out and consider diverse viewpoints
- Show appreciation for the strengths that diversity brings
2. **Addressing Biases**:
- Be aware of your own biases and work to mitigate them
- Encourage team members to examine their biases
3. **Creating Inclusion**:
- Ensure all team members feel valued and heard
- Adapt your communication style to different cultural norms

## Remote Leadership And Virtual Teams

Leading remote teams requires adapting EI strategies:

1. **Building Virtual Connection**:
- Use video calls to capture non-verbal cues
- Create opportunities for informal virtual interactions
2. **Engaging Remote Team Members**:
- Be more intentional about checking in on team members' wellbeing
- Use digital tools to facilitate collaboration and communication
3. **Adapting EI Strategies**:
- Be more explicit in your communication of emotions and expectations

- Pay extra attention to potential misunderstandings in digital communication

## Ethical Considerations In Emotionally Intelligent Leadership

Using EI ethically is crucial:

1. **Responsible Use of EI**:
   - Use your emotional understanding to benefit the team, not manipulate
   - Be transparent about your intentions and decision-making process
2. **Maintaining Authenticity**:
   - Align your actions with your values and stated principles
   - Encourage genuine emotional expression in your team
3. **Balancing Goals and Wellbeing**:
   - Consider both organizational objectives and employee welfare
   - Create a culture that values both performance and wellbeing

## Self-Care And Emotional Sustainability For Leaders

Leadership can be emotionally demanding. Practice self-care by:

1. **Managing Emotional Demands**:
   - Recognize the emotional labor involved in leadership
   - Develop strategies to recharge and maintain emotional balance
2. **Preventing Burnout**:
   - Set boundaries between work and personal life
   - Cultivate interests and relationships outside of work

3. **Continuous Improvement**:
   - Regularly reflect on your leadership practice
   - Seek feedback and be open to personal growth

Remember, taking care of yourself enables you to better care for your team.

## Measuring The Impact Of Emotionally Intelligent Leadership

Assess the effectiveness of your EI leadership:

   1. **Key Performance Indicators**:
   - Track metrics like team engagement, turnover, and performance
   - Look for improvements in team collaboration and innovation
   2. **Gathering Feedback**:
   - Use 360-degree feedback to get a comprehensive view
   - Encourage open, honest feedback from your team
   3. **Continuous Improvement**:
   - Regularly assess your EI skills and leadership effectiveness
   - Set personal development goals based on feedback and self-reflection

## Conclusion: Integrating Emotional Intelligence Into Your Leadership Identity

Leading with emotional intelligence is not about applying a set of techniques; it's about integrating EI into your leadership identity. It involves a commitment to self-awareness, continuous learning, and genuine care for your team members.

As you continue to develop your EI leadership skills, remember that this is an ongoing journey. Every interaction, decision, and challenge is an opportunity to apply and refine your emotional intelligence.

By leading with EI, you not only become a more effective leader but also create a more positive, productive, and fulfilling work environment for your entire team. You set the emotional tone for your organization, inspiring others to develop their own EI skills and contributing to a culture of empathy, understanding, and high performance.

In the next and final chapter, we'll explore how to create an emotionally intelligent workplace culture, extending the principles we've discussed throughout this book to the organizational level.

# CHAPTER 11

# Building an Emotionally Intelligent Workplace Culture

As we conclude our exploration of Emotional Intelligence (EI) in the workplace, we turn our attention to the broader organizational context. In this final chapter, we'll examine how to cultivate an emotionally intelligent workplace culture, one that not only supports but actively promotes the development and application of EI skills at all levels.

## Introduction To Emotionally Intelligent Organizations

An emotionally intelligent organization is one where EI is woven into the fabric of its culture, processes, and practices. Such organizations are characterized by:

- High levels of self-awareness and self-management among employees
- Strong interpersonal relationships and effective communication
- Adaptive and resilient responses to change and challenges

- A culture of trust, psychological safety, and continuous learning

The benefits of fostering EI at an organizational level are numerous:

- Improved employee engagement and job satisfaction
- Enhanced teamwork and collaboration
- Increased innovation and creativity
- Better customer relationships and service
- Higher overall performance and productivity

## Assessing The Current Emotional Climate Of Your Organization

Before embarking on a journey to build an EI culture, it's crucial to understand your starting point:

1. **Organizational EI Assessment Tools**:
   - Use validated EI assessment tools adapted for organizational use
   - Consider 360-degree feedback processes to get a comprehensive view
2. **Employee Surveys and Focus Groups**:
   - Gather qualitative data on employees' perceptions of the emotional climate
   - Explore areas like trust, communication, leadership, and workplace relationships
3. **Analyzing Existing Data**:
   - Review metrics like employee engagement scores, turnover rates, and performance data
   - Look for patterns that might indicate emotional intelligence strengths or deficits

Based on this assessment, identify your organization's EI strengths and areas for improvement.

## The Role Of Leadership In Creating An Emotionally Intelligent Culture

Leaders play a pivotal role in shaping organizational culture:

1. **Modeling EI Behaviors**:
   - Leaders must consistently demonstrate high EI in their interactions and decision-making
   - Be transparent about your own EI journey and challenges
2. **Championing EI Initiatives**:
   - Actively advocate for EI development programs and resources
   - Tie EI to organizational strategy and success
3. **Creating Accountability**:
   - Include EI competencies in leadership performance evaluations
   - Recognize and reward leaders who excel in fostering EI in their teams

Remember, a culture of EI must be cultivated from the top down as well as from the bottom up.

## Integrating Emotional Intelligence Into Organizational Values And Mission

To truly embed EI in your culture, it must be reflected in your core organizational identity:

1. **Aligning EI with Company Values**:
   - Review and revise company values to explicitly include EI principles
   - Ensure that EI-related values are clearly defined and actionable
2. **Communicating the Importance of EI**:

- Include EI in your mission statement and strategic plans
- Regularly communicate the role of EI in achieving organizational goals

3. **Living the Values**:
- Ensure that decision-making at all levels reflects EI values
- Share stories that highlight how EI contributes to organizational success

## Incorporating Emotional Intelligence Into Human Resources Practices

Human Resources plays a crucial role in institutionalizing EI:

1. **Recruitment and Selection**:
- Include EI competencies in job descriptions
- Use behavioral interview techniques to assess EI skills
- Consider EI assessments as part of the hiring process

2. **Performance Management**:
- Incorporate EI competencies into performance review criteria
- Provide training for managers on how to evaluate and discuss EI in performance conversations

3. **Compensation and Recognition**:
- Align reward systems to reinforce EI behaviors
- Recognize and celebrate examples of high EI in action

## Developing Emotional Intelligence Training And Development Programs

Systematic EI development is key to building an EI culture:

1. **Comprehensive EI Curricula**:
- Develop training programs that cover all aspects of EI
- Tailor programs for different organizational levels and

roles
2. **Ongoing Development Initiatives**:
   - Offer regular workshops, coaching, and peer learning opportunities
   - Create a resource library of EI materials and tools
3. **Measuring Effectiveness**:
   - Establish clear metrics for evaluating the impact of EI training
   - Continuously refine programs based on feedback and results

## Fostering Emotional Safety And Trust

An emotionally intelligent workplace is one where people feel safe to be authentic:

1. **Building Psychological Safety**:
   - Encourage risk-taking and viewing mistakes as learning opportunities
   - Create norms that support open and honest communication
2. **Encouraging Vulnerability**:
   - Leaders should model appropriate vulnerability
   - Celebrate instances where vulnerability leads to positive outcomes
3. **Conflict Resolution Processes**:
   - Establish clear, EI-based protocols for addressing conflicts
   - Train employees in constructive conflict resolution techniques

## Promoting Effective Communication Practices

Communication is at the heart of an EI culture:

1. **Establishing Communication Norms**:

- Create guidelines for respectful, empathetic communication
- Encourage active listening and checking for understanding
2. **Leveraging Technology**:
- Use digital tools that support emotional expression in remote work
- Provide training on maintaining EI in digital communication
3. **Regular Check-ins**:
- Implement practices like team mood check-ins or emotion-focused retrospectives
- Encourage frequent, informal feedback conversations

## Enhancing Team Dynamics Through Emotional Intelligence

Emotionally intelligent teams are the building blocks of an EI organization:

1. **Building EI Teams**:
- Consider EI skills when forming teams
- Provide team-based EI training and development
2. **Team-Building Activities**:
- Design activities that develop collective EI skills
- Use tools like emotion mapping for team projects
3. **Addressing Team Conflicts**:
- Teach teams to recognize and address emotional undercurrents
- Provide mediation resources for complex team dynamics

## Creating Emotionally Intelligent Policies And Procedures

Organizational policies should reflect and support EI principles:

1. **Policy Review**:
   - Audit existing policies for their emotional impact
   - Revise policies to better align with EI values
2. **Developing EI-Focused Procedures**:
   - Create procedures that consider emotional well-being (e.g., for giving feedback, managing performance issues)
   - Involve employees in developing these procedures to ensure they resonate
3. **Balancing Needs**:
   - Strive to create policies that balance organizational requirements with employee well-being
   - Be flexible and willing to adapt policies as needs evolve

## Nurturing Diversity, Equity, And Inclusion Through Emotional Intelligence

EI is a powerful tool for creating a more inclusive workplace:

1. **Addressing Bias**:
   Use EI training to help employees recognize and mitigate unconscious biases
   - Implement systems to identify and address microaggressions
2. **Fostering Cross-Cultural Empathy**:
   - Provide opportunities for cross-cultural learning and interaction
   - Use EI skills to navigate cultural differences respectfully
3. **Celebrating Diversity**:
   - Create platforms for sharing diverse experiences and perspectives
   - Ensure that diversity is reflected in leadership and decision-making processes

# Managing Change And Uncertainty With Emotional Intelligence

An EI culture is more resilient in the face of change:

1. **EI-Based Change Management**:
   o Incorporate emotional considerations into change plans
   o Provide emotional support resources during transitions
2. **Building Resilience**:
   o Offer training in emotional resilience and stress management
   o Create support networks to help employees navigate uncertainty
3. **Communicating Through Change**:
   o Use EI principles to guide communication during turbulent times
   o Be transparent about changes while acknowledging emotional impacts

# Measuring And Evaluating Emotional Intelligence Culture

Continuous assessment is crucial for maintaining and improving an EI culture:

1. **Developing EI Metrics**:
   o Create KPIs that reflect EI principles (e.g., psychological safety scores, empathy ratings)
   o Integrate EI measures into existing organizational health assessments
2. **Regular EI Audits**:
   o Conduct periodic, comprehensive reviews of organizational EI
   o Use a mix of quantitative and qualitative data to get a

full picture
3. **Data-Driven Improvement**:
   - Use assessment results to inform ongoing EI initiatives
   - Share progress and insights with the entire organization

## Overcoming Challenges In Building An Emotional Intelligence Culture

Creating an EI culture is not without its challenges:

1. **Addressing Resistance**:
   - Anticipate and plan for skepticism or resistance to EI initiatives
   - Use concrete examples and data to demonstrate the value of EI
2. **Resource Management**:
   - Make a clear business case for investing in EI development
   - Look for ways to integrate EI into existing processes to maximize resources
3. **Maintaining Momentum**:
   - Develop a long-term strategy for sustaining EI focus
   - Regularly renew and refresh EI initiatives to keep engagement high

## The Future Of Emotionally Intelligent Workplaces

As we look ahead, several trends are shaping the future of EI in organizations:

1. **AI and EI:**
   - Explore how AI can support EI development and application
   - Consider the ethical implications of AI in emotional contexts

2. **Evolving Workplace Demands**:
   - Prepare for increased emphasis on adaptability and resilience
   - Consider how changing work models (e.g., remote, hybrid) impact EI needs
3. **Personalized EI Development**:
   - Leverage technology for more personalized, on-demand EI learning
   - Explore emerging tools for real-time EI coaching and feedback

## Action Plan For Creating An Emotionally Intelligent Workplace

To begin your organization's EI transformation:

1. **Assess**: Conduct a comprehensive EI assessment of your organization
2. **Align**: Ensure leadership is aligned and committed to EI culture development
3. **Educate**: Begin with broad EI education to create a common language and understanding
4. **Integrate**: Systematically integrate EI into HR processes, policies, and daily operations
5. **Develop**: Implement ongoing EI development programs at all levels
6. **Measure**: Regularly assess progress and adjust strategies as needed
7. **Reinforce**: Continuously communicate the importance of EI and celebrate EI wins

## Conclusion: The Transformative Power Of Emotional Intelligence In The Workplace

As we conclude this book, it's clear that emotional intelligence is not just a nice-to-have skill set, but a fundamental requirement for success in the modern workplace. By cultivating EI at both individual and organizational levels, we create environments where people can thrive, innovate, and perform at their best.

Building an emotionally intelligent workplace is a journey, not a destination. It requires ongoing commitment, effort, and adaptation. But the rewards – in terms of employee well-being, organizational performance, and societal impact – are immeasurable.

As you move forward in your EI journey, remember that every interaction, decision, and policy is an opportunity to reinforce and deepen your organization's emotional intelligence. By doing so, you're not just creating a better workplace; you're contributing to a more empathetic, understanding, and effective world.

Thank you for joining us on this exploration of Emotional Intelligence in the workplace. May your path forward be filled with growth, connection, and success.

# REFERENCE

# Self-Regulation Techniques and How to Perform Them

## Box Breathing Technique: A Comprehensive Guide

### What Is Box Breathing?

Box breathing is a simple yet powerful relaxation technique that can help reduce stress, improve focus, and restore calm. It's called "box" breathing because the pattern of inhaling, holding, exhaling, and holding again follows a 4-4-4-4 count, creating a mental picture of a square or box.

### How To Perform Box Breathing

1. **Find a Comfortable Position:**
   - Sit upright in a comfortable chair with your feet flat on the ground.
   - You can also lie down if that's more comfortable.
2. **Exhale Completely:**
   - Begin by exhaling all the air from your lungs.
3. **Inhale:**
   - Slowly inhale through your nose for a count of 4.

- Focus on filling your lungs from the bottom up.
4. **Hold**:
   - Hold your breath for a count of 4.
   - Keep your muscles relaxed.
5. **Exhale**:
   - Slowly exhale through your mouth for a count of 4.
   - Try to exhale completely.
6. **Hold**:
   - Hold your breath again for a count of 4 before starting the next cycle.
7. **Repeat**:
   - Continue this pattern for at least 4-5 cycles, or until you feel calm and centered.

## Tips For Effective Practice

- Maintain a steady rhythm. It may help to visualize tracing the outline of a square as you breathe.
- If 4 seconds feels too long or short, adjust the count to what feels comfortable for you. The key is to keep all four phases equal in duration.
- Practice when you're calm to make it easier to use when you're stressed.
- Use this technique before stressful events, during moments of tension, or as a daily relaxation practice.

## Benefits Of Box Breathing

- Reduces stress and anxiety
- Improves focus and concentration
- Helps manage emotional responses
- Can lower blood pressure
- Promotes relaxation and better sleep

## When To Use Box Breathing

1. Before important meetings or presentations
2. During conflict or tense situations at work
3. When feeling overwhelmed or anxious
4. As part of a daily mindfulness routine
5. To refocus during long work sessions

## The 5-4-3-2-1 Grounding Technique: A Comprehensive Guide

### What Is The 5-4-3-2-1 Grounding Technique?

The 5-4-3-2-1 technique is a grounding exercise that uses your five senses to help you shift your focus away from distressing thoughts and center yourself in the present moment. This method can be particularly effective for managing anxiety, stress, and overwhelming emotions.

### How To Perform The 5-4-3-2-1 Technique

1. **Find a Comfortable Position**:
- Sit or stand in a comfortable position.
- Take a deep, calming breath to begin.
2. **5 Things You Can See**:
- Look around you and name five things you can see.
- These can be objects, colors, or details in your environment.
- Example: "I see my computer screen, a blue pen, a plant, the clock on the wall, and my coffee mug."
3. **4 Things You Can Touch**:

- Name four things you can physically feel or touch.
 - These can be textures, temperatures, or sensations.
 - Example: "I can feel the smooth surface of my desk, the fabric of my shirt, the coolness of the air conditioning, and the firmness of the chair I'm sitting on."
4. **3 Things You Can Hear**:
 - Identify three sounds you can hear around you.
 - Try to notice sounds you might usually tune out.
 - Example: "I can hear the hum of my computer, people talking in the hallway, and the sound of traffic outside."
5. **2 Things You Can Smell**:
 - Name two scents you can smell.
 - If you can't smell anything at the moment, think of two favorite smells.
 - Example: "I can smell coffee and the scent of my hand lotion."
6. **1 Thing You Can Taste**:
 - Identify one thing you can taste right now.
 - If you can't taste anything, name a favorite taste.
 - Example: "I can taste the mint from my chewing gum."
7. **Reflect**:
 - Take another deep breath and notice how you feel after completing the exercise.

## Tips For Effective Practice

- Practice this technique when you're calm to make it easier to use in stressful moments.
- Customize the order or number of senses based on what works best for you.
- Use descriptive language to engage more fully with each sensation.
- If you're in a situation where you can't speak aloud, go through the steps silently in your mind.

## Benefits Of The 5-4-3-2-1 Technique

- Quickly reduces anxiety and stress
- Helps manage panic attacks
- Improves focus and concentration
- Brings attention to the present moment
- Can be done discreetly in any environment

## When To Use The 5-4-3-2-1 Technique In The Workplace

- Before important presentations or meetings
- During moments of high stress or anxiety
- When feeling overwhelmed by tasks or deadlines
- To refocus after a difficult interaction
- As a quick break during long work sessions

Remember, the key to this technique is engaging your senses to ground yourself in the present moment. With practice, it can become a powerful tool for managing stress and maintaining emotional balance in the workplace.

## Progressive Muscle Relaxation: A Comprehensive Guide

## What Is Progressive Muscle Relaxation?

Progressive Muscle Relaxation (PMR) is a relaxation technique that involves systematically tensing and then relaxing different muscle groups in the body. This method helps you become more aware of physical tension and provides a way to release that tension, promoting physical and mental relaxation.

## How To Perform Progressive Muscle Relaxation

1. **Prepare**:
   - Find a quiet, comfortable place where you won't be disturbed.
   - Sit in a comfortable chair or lie down.
   - Loosen any tight clothing.
2. **Begin with Breathing**:
   - Take a few deep, slow breaths to start relaxing.
3. **Focus on Muscle Groups**:
   - Work through each muscle group in sequence, typically starting from the feet and moving up to the head.
4. **Tension and Relaxation Cycle**:
   - For each muscle group: a. Tense the muscles as tightly as you can for about 5 seconds. b. Release the tension suddenly and completely. c. Relax the muscles for about 10-15 seconds. d. Notice the difference between tension and relaxation.
5. **Muscle Group Sequence**:
   - Feet: Curl your toes tightly into your feet, then release.
   - Calves: Point or flex your feet, then relax.
   - Thighs: Squeeze your thighs together, then relax.
   - Hips and buttocks: Tighten this area, then release.
   - Stomach: Suck your stomach in, then relax.
   - Chest: Tighten your chest muscles, then release.
   - Back: Arch your back, then relax.
   - Arms and hands: Make fists and tense your arms, then relax.
   - Shoulders: Shrug your shoulders up to your ears, then drop them.
   - Face: Scrunch your facial muscles, then relax.
   - Jaw: Clench your jaw, then release.
6. **Final Relaxation**:
   - After completing all muscle groups, remain in a relaxed

state for a few minutes.
  - Focus on the feeling of relaxation throughout your body.

## Tips For Effective Practice

- Maintain focus on the distinction between tension and relaxation.
- Don't tense to the point of pain or cramping.
- Breathe normally throughout the exercise.
- Practice regularly for best results, ideally daily.
- You can record the instructions to guide yourself through the process.

## Benefits Of Progressive Muscle Relaxation

- Reduces overall body tension
- Alleviates anxiety and stress
- Improves sleep quality
- Helps with headaches and other tension-related pain
- Increases awareness of physical stress signals
- Enhances overall sense of well-being and calm

## When To Use Progressive Muscle Relaxation In The Workplace

- Before important meetings or presentations to reduce nervousness
- During lunch breaks to reset and refresh
- After a stressful interaction to release tension
- At the end of the workday to transition from work to personal time
- As part of a regular stress management routine

## Adapting Progressive Muscle Relaxation For The

## Workplace

- Practice a shortened version focusing on key areas like shoulders, jaw, and hands.
- Use discreet techniques like clenching and releasing your fists under a desk.
- Incorporate brief relaxation moments throughout your day, even if you can't do the full sequence.

Remember, Progressive Muscle Relaxation becomes more effective with regular practice. As you become more familiar with the technique, you'll be able to relax your muscles more quickly and easily, even in challenging workplace situations.

## Cognitive Reframing: A Comprehensive Guide

## What Is Cognitive Reframing?

Cognitive Reframing, also known as cognitive restructuring, is a psychological technique used to identify and challenge negative or irrational thought patterns and replace them with more balanced, realistic perspectives. It's a core component of Cognitive Behavioral Therapy (CBT) and can be a powerful tool for managing stress, anxiety, and negative emotions in various settings, including the workplace.

## How To Practice Cognitive Reframing

1. **Identify the Situation:**
   - Recognize a situation that's causing you distress or negative emotions.
2. **Notice Your Automatic Thoughts**:
   - Pay attention to the immediate thoughts that come to

mind in response to the situation.
   - These are often automatic and may not be entirely rational.
3. **Identify Cognitive Distortions**:
   - Look for common thinking traps such as:
     - All-or-nothing thinking
     - Overgeneralization
     - Catastrophizing
     - Mind reading
     - Should statements
     - Personalization
4. **Challenge Your Thoughts**:
   - Ask yourself:
     - Is this thought based on facts or assumptions?
     - Am I overlooking any positive aspects?
     - How would I advise a friend in this situation?
     - What's the worst that could happen? How likely is it?
     - Will this matter in a year from now?
5. **Generate Alternative Perspectives**:
   - Try to come up with at least three alternative ways of viewing the situation.
   - Focus on more balanced, realistic interpretations.
6. **Choose a New Perspective**:
   - Select the most realistic and helpful perspective.
   - It doesn't have to be overly positive, just more balanced than the original thought.
7. **Reflect on the New Perspective**:
   - Notice how the new perspective affects your emotions and behavior.

# Example Of Cognitive Reframing In A Workplace Context

Original Situation: You make a mistake during a presentation.

Automatic Thought: "I'm a complete failure. Everyone thinks I'm incompetent now."

Reframed Perspective: "Making a mistake doesn't define my entire performance or career. Everyone makes mistakes sometimes, and this is an opportunity to learn and improve."

## Tips For Effective Practice

- Practice regularly, not just in high-stress situations.
- Keep a thought journal to track patterns in your thinking.
- Be patient with yourself; changing thought patterns takes time.
- Seek professional help if you're struggling with persistent negative thoughts.

## Benefits Of Cognitive Reframing

- Reduces stress and anxiety
- Improves problem-solving skills
- Enhances emotional regulation
- Boosts resilience and adaptability
- Increases overall job satisfaction and performance

## When To Use Cognitive Reframing In The Workplace

- Before important meetings or presentations to manage nervousness
- After receiving critical feedback to maintain a growth mindset
- When facing challenging projects or deadlines
- During conflicts with colleagues to maintain perspective
- In times of organizational change to adapt more easily

## Strategies For Implementing Cognitive Reframing At Work

1. **Pause and Reflect**: When you notice negative emotions, take a moment to identify your thoughts.
2. **Use "I" Statements**: Frame your thoughts as "I" statements to take ownership and make them easier to challenge.
3. **Look for Evidence**: Seek out facts that support or contradict your thoughts.
4. **Consider Multiple Perspectives**: Try to view the situation from different angles, including those of your colleagues or supervisors.
5. **Focus on Growth**: Reframe challenges as opportunities for learning and development.
6. **Practice Self-Compassion**: Treat yourself with the same kindness you would offer a colleague.

Remember, cognitive reframing is a skill that improves with practice. By consistently applying this technique, you can create a more positive, resilient mindset that will serve you well in all aspects of your professional life.

## Mindfulness Meditation And Emotional Labeling: A Comprehensive Guide

# Mindfulness Meditation

## What Is Mindfulness Meditation?

Mindfulness meditation is a practice that involves focusing your attention on the present moment, acknowledging and accepting your thoughts, feelings, and bodily sensations without judgment.

It's rooted in Buddhist traditions but has been widely adopted in Western psychology and wellness practices.

## How to Practice Mindfulness Meditation

1. **Find a Comfortable Position:**
   - Sit in a chair or on the floor, keeping your back straight but not stiff.
   - You can also lie down if that's more comfortable.
2. **Set a Time Limit:**
   - Begin with 5-10 minutes and gradually increase as you become more comfortable.
3. **Focus on Your Breath:**
   - Pay attention to the sensation of breathing in and out.
   - Notice the rise and fall of your chest or the air moving through your nostrils.
4. **Notice When Your Mind Wanders:**
   - It's natural for thoughts to arise. When you notice this happening, gently redirect your attention back to your breath.
   - Don't judge yourself for getting distracted; simply return to your focus.
5. **Be Kind to Your Wandering Mind:**
   - Treat the process of returning to your breath as a skill you're developing, not a task at which to succeed or fail.
6. **End the Session Gently:**
   - When your time is up, slowly open your eyes if they were closed.
   - Take a moment to notice how you feel before moving on with your day.

## Benefits of Mindfulness Meditation

- Reduces stress and anxiety
- Improves focus and concentration
- Enhances emotional regulation
- Increases self-awareness

- Promotes overall well-being

## Applying Mindfulness in the Workplace

- Practice a brief meditation before starting your workday
- Use mindful breathing during stressful moments
- Incorporate mindfulness into your lunch break
- Practice mindful listening during meetings
- Use mindfulness to transition between tasks

# Emotional Labeling

## What is Emotional Labeling?

Emotional labeling is the practice of identifying and naming your emotions as you experience them. This technique helps create a psychological distance between you and your emotions, allowing for better understanding and management of your feelings.

## How to Practice Emotional Labeling

1. **Pause and Reflect**:
   - When you notice a strong emotion, take a moment to pause.
2. **Identify the Emotion**:
   - Try to name the specific emotion you're feeling.
   - Be as precise as possible (e.g., "frustrated" instead of just "upset").
3. **Verbalize or Write It Down**:
   - Say the emotion out loud or write it down: "I am feeling [emotion]."
4. **Acknowledge Physical Sensations**:
   - Notice how the emotion manifests in your body (e.g., tightness in chest, clenched jaw).
5. **Avoid Judgment**:
   - Accept the emotion without criticizing yourself for feeling it.

6. **Investigate the Cause**:
   - Reflect on what might have triggered this emotion.
7. **Choose a Response**:
   - Now that you've labeled the emotion, consider how you want to respond to the situation.

## Benefits of Emotional Labeling

- Reduces the intensity of negative emotions
- Improves emotional self-awareness
- Enhances decision-making in emotional situations
- Facilitates better communication about feelings
- Helps in developing emotional intelligence

## Applying Emotional Labeling in the Workplace

- Use labeling to process emotions before important meetings
- Practice labeling during conflict resolution
- Incorporate emotional labeling into performance reviews (both giving and receiving)
- Use labeling to manage stress during high-pressure projects
- Apply labeling when receiving feedback to maintain objectivity

## Combining Mindfulness and Emotional Labeling

Mindfulness meditation and emotional labeling can be powerful when used together:

1. Begin with a short mindfulness practice to center yourself.
2. As you meditate, notice any emotions that arise.
3. Label these emotions as they appear, without getting caught up in them.
4. Return your focus to your breath after labeling.

This combined approach can significantly enhance your emotional awareness and regulation skills, leading to better stress management and interpersonal relationships in the workplace.

Remember, both mindfulness meditation and emotional labeling are skills that improve with practice. Regular, consistent practice, even for short periods, can lead to significant benefits in your personal and professional life.